A Guide to the
National Curriculum

Bob Moon is Professor of Education at the Open University.

From reviews of earlier editions:

'clear, comprehensive . . . essential for the staffroom shelf'
Juliet Hobson, *Times Educational Supplement*

'. . . Parents and governors should certainly find it
informative . . . up-to-date [and] readable'
Michael Salter, *Education*

A Guide to the
National Curriculum

THIRD EDITION

Bob Moon

OXFORD UNIVERSITY PRESS

Oxford University Press, Walton Street, Oxford OX2 6DP

Oxford New York
Athens Auckland Bangkok Bombay
Calcutta Cape Town Dar es Salaam Delhi
Florence Hong Kong Istanbul Karachi
Kuala Lumpur Madras Madrid Melbourne
Mexico City Nairobi Paris Singapore
Taipei Tokyo Toronto

and associated companies in
Berlin Ibadan

Oxford is a trade mark of Oxford University Press

First published as an Oxford University Press paperback 1991
Second edition 1994
Third edition 1996

British Library Cataloguing in Publication Data
Data available

Library of Congress Cataloging in Publication Data
Moon, Bob.
   A guide to the national curriculum / Bob Moon. — 3rd ed.
   Includes bibliographical references (p.   ).
   1. Education—Great Britain—Curricula.   I. Title.
  LB1564.G7M66 1996
  375'.00941—dc20   95–31901

ISBN 0–19–288007–1

10 9 8 7 6 5 4

Printed in Great Britain by
Biddles Ltd.,
Guildford and King's Lynn

Preface

A wide range of people have contributed to the information and ideas contained within this guide, which is now in a third edition. Officers from the National Councils have been helpful at each stage. Keith Hedger and Michael Raleigh of Shropshire LEA provided detailed comments on the first edition. My colleagues in the Open University School of Education have looked at different parts of the guide in detail and in places provided draft text for me to integrate into the guide. I would like, therefore, to thank particularly:

Frank Banks
Hilary Bourdillon
Jill Bourne
Sue Brindley
Jenny Leach
Ralph Levinson
Jane Maybin
Patricia Murphy

Michelle Selinger
Ann Shelton
Christine Shiu
Charles Sproule
Gary Spruce
Will Swann
Ann Swarbrick

Dorothy Calderwood, Elizabeth Freeman, and Julie Herbert have provided the necessary administrative and secretarial support. Finally I would like to thank Barbara Vander, who first suggested that a guide such as this would be of interest and value to those coming new to the national curriculum.

B.M.

Oxford
April 1995

Contents

Introduction

The National Curriculum, introduced in 1988 as part of the Education Reform Act, represents one of the most significant educational reforms this century. It is a public statement about the syllabus and content that every child should study until he or she leaves school. It is important for teachers and parents to understand the structure and terminology of the curriculum as a whole and the individual subjects within it. This is particularly so for teachers in training and for the thousands of parents playing an active role on governing bodies and parent–teacher associations.

This guide:

- provides an introduction to the way the national curriculum is organized in primary, secondary, and middle schools;
- explains the meanings of the terms used on a daily basis now by teachers and by pupils;
- outlines the content of the different subjects;
- gives guidance on the systems of assessment and testing used;
- sets out the entitlement parents have in relation to their child's progress;
- explores a number of the controversial issues associated with the early years of National Curriculum development in schools.

In using this guide, two important points need to be borne in mind. First, it does not attempt to serve as a substitute for the statutory orders, official regulations, and formal documentation associated with the National Curriculum. Some of the documentation is daunting, even for the interested reader, but it does prescribe the legal basis upon which the National Curriculum is based. Regular changes have occurred in the content of some of the subjects, and the way testing and assessment is organized, and it is necessary to refer to the official publications for the precise legal situation at any one time or in respect of a particular age group. These publications are quite expensive, but all schools keep copies and can make them available to parents. It is especially important to note that in Wales and in Northern Ireland there are differences from the prescribed arrangements in England. The terminology and the organization around key stages remain the same but the organization and content of some subjects do vary. In Northern Ireland, for example, the statutory National Curriculum is set out in terms of five areas of study: English, mathematics, science and technology, environment and society, and creative and expansive studies. The National Curriculum in Northern Ireland has undergone a revision process similar to that carried out for England and Wales. This was incomplete at the time this third edition went to press. This leads to a second point. The information and guidance set out in this guide are supplemented by contact and involvement with schools. Early experience with the National Curriculum has shown that schools require greater flexibility than was envisaged in 1988, and changes have been introduced to permit this. A review of the National Curriculum carried out by Sir Ron Dearing, chairman of the Schools Curriculum and Assessment Authority (SCAA), led to changes to the legal requirements in each of the subjects and the way these are assessed. A radically restructured National Curriculum was introduced in September 1995 (September 1996 for those taking GCSE examinations), with the expectation that this would remain substantially the same for at least five years. Despite the political and educational difficulties in introducing the National Curriculum, a central core of curriculum opportunities and entitlement for all children is now enshrined in law. There is political support for this across all major political parties. The National Curriculum will be one of the corner-stones of school development in the 1990s and through to the twenty-first century. This guide is a contribution to ensuring that it is appreciated and understood by everyone with an interest and involvement in education.

1 What is the National Curriculum?

In order to understand the National Curriculum, you will first need to become familiar with a small number of terms and phrases. These are straightforward not only for teachers, governors, and parents but also, perhaps with the exception of the very youngest, for pupils in schools.

The National Curriculum forms an important part of the Education Reform Act that became law in the summer of 1988. The aims of the new curriculum, set out in Clause 2, are to prescribe a number of school subjects and specify in relation to each:

- the knowledge, skills, and understanding which pupils of different abilities and maturities are expected to have;
- the matters, skills, and processes which are required to be taught to pupils of different abilities and maturities;
- arrangements for assessing pupils.

Key Stages

The National Curriculum must be taught to pupils in all maintained schools or local authority schools as well as in grant-maintained schools. It also applies to special schools within both these sectors. It is organized on the basis of four key stages:

	Pupil's ages	*Year groups*
Key Stage 1	5–7	1–2
Key Stage 2	7–11	3–6
Key Stage 3	11–14	7–9
Key Stage 4	14–16	10–11

The phrase *key stage* is now used frequently by teachers, for example, when explaining to new parents how the curriculum of the school is organized.

Core and other foundation subjects

The National Curriculum is described as ten subjects. Three of the subjects are defined as *core foundation* subjects and seven as *foundation* subjects. Most of the subjects are well known and have featured in the school curriculum for many years.

Core foundation subjects[1]	English, mathematics, science
Foundation subjects	Art, geography, history, modern languages, music, physical education, technology

The original plan was to teach all ten subjects through to the age of 16, with the exception of modern languages, which would only be introduced at the secondary 11+ age-group.

This proved to be too inflexible for the post-14 year-old age group where greater choice has traditionally been allowed. The minimum statutory, legal requirement that maintained schools must provide post-14 teaching in English, mathematics, science, physical education, information technology, design and technology, and a modern foreign language. Not all of this, however, needs to be taken as a full GCSE. Shorter courses in design and technology and a modern foreign language are allowed.

The National Curriculum for England is published in one composite document, as well as separately for each subject, by Her Majesty's Stationery Office (see Further Reading). These documents cover the period up to the end of Year 9 in the secondary school; thereafter the National Curriculum is mostly covered by GCSE Examination syllabus. In Wales and Northern Ireland equivalent publications are available.

Schools are required, as they always have been, to teach religious education. However, this is not one of the ten subjects of the National

---

[1] In Wales, Welsh is also taught as a core foundation subject where the medium of instruction in the schools is Welsh. In all other Welsh schools it is one of the foundation subjects.

Curriculum, and arrangements for drawing up an agreed syllabus are made at the local-education-authority, not national, level.

In the way the National Curriculum has developed there is little legal distinction between the core foundation and foundation subjects. The secretary of state was required to introduce the three core subjects before any others, but the way the content is described is the same for each of the ten subjects. Three terms are used to describe each subject:

- programmes of study;
- attainment targets;
- level descriptions.

Programmes of study

The ways in which the attainment targets and statements of attainment are to be taught are set out in *programmes of study* (PoS). Teachers and schools are bound to follow these; they give more information to teachers about contents, methods, and approaches.

The programmes of study cover skills that need to be developed and the knowledge and content essential to understanding a subject. In geography, for example, 11–14 year-olds should, in investigating places and themes, be given opportunities to:

a   identify geographical questions and issues and establish an appropriate sequence of investigation;

b   identify the evidence required and collect, record, and present it;

c   analyse and evaluate the evidence, draw conclusions, and communicate findings.

In looking at places to study the geography curriculum must include countries other than the United Kingdom for this age group, and teachers are given the choice within each of two lists:

List A	*List B*
Australia and New Zealand	Africa
Europe	Asia (excluding Japan)
Japan	South and Central America
North America	(including the Caribbean)
Russian Federation	

Attainment targets and level descriptions

National Curriculum attainment targets set out the expected standards of pupils' performance when that part of the Programme of Study has been completed. The attainment targets (ATs), therefore, are an important basis for teachers assessments and any national tests that might be taken.

Some subjects have more than one attainment target. In mathematics, for example, there are four:

AT1. Using and Applying Mathematics;
AT2. Numbers and Algebra;
AT3. Shapes, Space, and Measure;
AT4. Handling data.

In other subjects, geography for example, the subject title is the attainment target. For all attainment targets there are a series of *level descriptions*. This is where the terms begin to sound like educational jargon! It is, however, a straightforward concept. Each attainment target is divided into eight levels. Level 1 is the first that a child would try to achieve after a short time in primary school. Level 8 is the standard you would expect of a 14 year-old. There is also an additional level description beyond 8—it has no number—which allows teachers to set further targets for those pupils doing exceptionally well in the subject. Each attainment target, therefore, represents something akin to a 'ladder' that shows the progress that pupils make as they move through the curriculum. In geography, for example, the Level 6 description reads as follows.

Level 6

Pupils show their knowledge, understanding and skills in relation to a wide range of studies of places and themes, at various scales. They explain a range of physical and human processes. They describe ways in which processes operating at different scales create geographical patterns and lead to changes in places. They describe and offer explanations for different approaches to managing environments and appreciate that different approaches have different effects on people and places. Drawing on their knowledge and understanding, pupils identify relevant geographical questions and suggest appropriate sequences of investigation. They select and make effective use of a wide range of skills, from the Key Stage 3 programme of study, and evidence in carrying out investigations. They present conclusions that are consistent with the evidence.

The language is rather formal. Those who wrote the attainment targets were trying to establish statements which precisely describe what pupils should be able to do. It does not read easily but it does allow teachers to think more clearly about the tasks they are set in the classroom. It allows them, for example, to assess whether a pupil really can 'explain a range of physical and human processes'. To understand what a pupil should be studying in school you need first to look at the programmes of study. To appreciate more clearly the focus of assessment, whether by teachers, or in some subjects by externally set national tests, you need to refer to the attainment targets and the descriptions of the eight levels that cover all the primary years and the 11–14 age range of the secondary school. Pupils will, of course, progress at different rates and it is necessary to talk to class or subject teachers to determine precisely which level they will be aiming for in the different subjects. As a rule of thumb the majority of pupils will reach level 3 during Key Stage 1 (5–7 years), level 5/6 by the end of Key Stage 2 (7–11 years), and levels 7 or 8 by Key Stage 3 (11–14 years). The ladder structure of the National Curriculum does allow some pupils to progress more quickly, perhaps in a subject where they have a particular aptitude. For others, who need to take a longer time over the earlier stages of work, it may be necessary to go more slowly through the different levels.

Not all the National Curriculum subjects have eight level descriptions. It was decided that for art, music, and physical education the detail that goes with eight levels would be unnecessary. In these subject areas teacher assessment is more general and the descriptions of attainment have only been provided at the end of each Key Stage. Below, for example, is the level description for the end of Key Stage 1 in physical education. Pupils at around 7 should be able to:

plan and perform simple skills safely, and show control in linking actions together. They improve their performance through practising their skills, working alone and with a partner. They talk about what they and others have done, and are able to make simple judgements. They recognize and describe the changes that happen to their bodies during exercise.

This reads, as already indicated, rather formally, but it is primarily designed to guide teachers in making judgements about the standards achieved. There are no national tests in physical education. The programme of study for the subject, however, offers a rich and diverse range of ways in which these standards can be achieved, including games, gymnastics, and dance and for parents this provides the best guide to what is happening in school.

The curriculum as a whole

The Education Reform Act does not lay down how long or for what percentage of the week the prescribed subjects should be studied. The revised National Curriculum, introduced in 1995, contains less content than earlier models to allow the release of at least one day a week in Key Stages 1–3 and to permit schools and teachers to develop curriculum activities outside those now required by law.

The Education Reform Act also does not lay down for how long or for what percentage of the week each subject should be studied. Subsequent regulations only talk of providing a reasonable amount of time, which permits schools to organize their schemes of work to allow for worthwhile study by each pupil of the knowledge, skills, and understanding, including processes, normally associated with the foundation subjects.

There has been much speculation about how time is best divided up, especially at the upper secondary level, where the timetable usually allows a certain percentage of time (about 10 per cent) for each subject and half that for short courses. Responsibility for these decisions lies with the school and in particular with the governing board. It is wise to check the curriculum arrangements for Key Stage 4 with the school or the local education authority.

It is important to remember that schools do not have to teach in subjects. Very few, if any, primary schools divide the school week up into ten or eleven subjects, and many secondary schools combine certain subject areas for teaching purposes. History and geography, for example, may become humanities; music and art may be part of the overall arts provision that includes dance and drama. This poses no difficulties, and may have certain advantages as long as attention is given to the content of the National Curriculum subject areas, and provided, where programmes of study are laid down in statutory orders, that the requirements are met. There are many ways in which schools can set out to do this. The particular style and approach chosen has to be agreed by the school governors, who in turn report to parents. Information about the curriculum must also be given in the school prospectus. Chapter 8 explains these requirements in some detail.

The information given to parents may include a section of what schools term 'cross curriculum planning'. This may include topics such as careers education or study skills which may not appear in the Programme of Study of the National Curriculum because they are taught through a range of subjects.

A final point

The National Curriculum lays down no requirements about the methods teachers should use. There is often debate around this subject but that is something that individual schools with the governing body need to decide. The Schools Curriculum and Assessment Authority (SCAA), the agency responsible in England for advising the government on the National Curriculum, is very clear on this point. In the introduction to the Revised National Curriculum, produced in 1995, it was clearly stated:

How and in what depth to teach the material contained in the subject Orders is for schools to decide. No priority or methodology is implied in the Orders. Decisions on the depth of treatment of aspects of subjects are for the professional judgement of teachers. The Orders should not be over-interpreted as requiring teaching to the same degree of detail in all aspects.

2 Why a National Curriculum?

Advocates of a National Curriculum can be found right across the political spectrum, and it is now clear that a National Curriculum will be part of the educational scene for the foreseeable future.

Differences between schools

For many educationists the logic that underpins the provision of free and compulsory schooling also extends to what is taught. In arguing for a National Curriculum, they point to glaring inconsistencies that used to exist between schools. In the same locality, one primary school might have had a fully worked-out science scheme, and another school no science scheme at all. Even if both schools did have plans for teaching science, there would be no guarantee that they would approach the subject in similar ways. One school might have attempted to achieve a balance between the different scientific disciplines (physics, chemistry, biology, and perhaps astronomy and earth sciences). The other, however, could have leaned heavily on the tradition of nature study—the sort of primary science that most parents remember from their own school-days. In other subjects similar differences existed. A survey by Her Majesty's Inspectorate at the end of the 1980s showed how haphazard the teaching of history and geography could be. It pointed to the lack of any attempt in many schools to ensure that children came into contact with progressively more demanding ideas, skills, and concepts.

Inequality of provision

In secondary schools the existence of different curriculum opportunities could be seen clearly. Girls, for example, often chose to drop the physical sciences in favour of biology. Boys significantly outnumbered girls in the technology classes that became increasingly available in the decade prior to the passing of the 1988 Education Reform Act. In a similar way, boys had very little contact with home economics. The number of students opting to study modern languages through to the end of year 11 or 13 was considerably less than in other subjects, and overall standards naturally appeared lower than in many other European countries. A National Curriculum provides a framework that could rule out such inconsistencies and inequalities.

Raising standards

Many supporters of the National Curriculum were also motivated by the desire to improve the quality of schooling and raise standards. The debate over standards has attracted media interest and controversy for many years. Some people have perceived a fall in standards of attainment in subjects such as English and mathematics. This is vigorously refuted by others, who point to the regular improvements in examination performance of both 16- and 18-year-olds. Each year the publication of GCSE and A-level results receives national attention and, overall, in each year there has been a gradual improvement in standards. About half of all the GCSE subjects taken are now graded at the higher level A–C. At 'A' level over a third of school-leavers are now obtaining the grades to go on to University; thirty years ago it was less than 10 per cent.

Judging standards over time is a complex task. Knowledge is always evolving and the sorts of tasks and questions that are appropriate in one decade may be redundant in the next. Extending the comparisons over more than a decade gives even greater difficulties. Changes in language usage make comparisons in English difficult. In mathematics the pound, shillings, and pence sums familiar to some parents and grandparents could hardly be set today.

Despite the complexity and inconclusiveness of the debate, a political and media message about declining standards achieved widespread public acceptance. More than one prime minister has chosen to exploit the issue for political advantage. James Callaghan, in a famous speech at Ruskin College, Oxford, in 1976, talked of his concern at finding 'complaints from industry that new recruits from the schools sometimes do not have the basic tools to do the job that is required'. Margaret Thatcher in her 1987 speech to the Conservative Party Conference made a direct link between schooling and economic success: 'To compete successfully in tomorrow's world—against Japan, Germany and the United States—we need well-educated, well-trained, creative young people. If education is backward today, the national performance will be backward tomorrow.' In the 1980s and 1990s education seemed the No. 1 priority for whoever was prime minister!

International comparisons represent a further dimension of the standards debate. Yet again, there are difficulties in coming to conclusive judgements. Setting tests that are comparable across a range of different countries and cultures has proved highly controversial. Assessments of practical and investigative work in science, for example, increasingly a feature of British science education, would be inappropriate in a different educational system where most teaching was through books and academic exercises. Some comparisons have been made that show how in mathematics and some aspects of science British pupils do not attain such high standards as their Japanese equivalents. A publication by the International Associates for the Evaluation of Educational Achievement, *Science Achievement in Seventeen Countries*, showed that this was particularly true in the initial stages of secondary education, where England is listed with Hong Kong, Italy, Singapore, and the USA. These are all countries which the report says should be concerned about 'the scientific literacy of their general workforce'. Finland, Hungary, Japan, and Sweden led the field in mass secondary science attainment. The same report, however, shows that at more advanced levels Hong Kong, England, and Singapore together with Hungary and Japan would appear to be educating their élites relatively well.

There arises from this a recurring message for schools in England, Wales, and Northern Ireland (Scotland, with a separate education system, does not have a statutory National Curriculum). Traditionally, the higher-attaining pupils can hold their own with the best in the world. But as we move into the twenty-first century these standards need deepening to cover a much wider range of pupils. The jobs of the twenty-first century will require much higher levels of skill and knowledge than those of the twentieth. The key issue is not whether standards are falling, but whether they are rising fast enough.

A great deal of evidence suggests the rather common-sense idea that people respond to the expectations you have of them. In school this is especially true. The National Curriculum defines what the vast majority of pupils should know at certain ages and, over time, this could contribute significantly to raising standards.

Improving communication

Creating a curriculum entitlement and raising standards are the two major justifications for a prescribed National Curriculum. There are, however, further supporting arguments. Many parents have found the curriculum a rather obscure part of the school's activities. There is research evidence and, again, a good deal of common-sense support for the view that the more parents know about what their children are expected to learn and achieve, the more likely the children are to succeed. Information such as this has been difficult for parents to obtain, not because of any obstruction on the part of teachers, but because there was no common language or agreed structure within which to explain or report on children's progress. Even where examination syllabuses existed, for GCSE or A level, for example, parents could find it difficult to ascertain even roughly what point in the syllabus their child had reached. In many instances pupils would sit the examination without ever having seen the syllabus. The National Curriculum, with its relatively straightforward terminology, provides the basis for greater clarity in school–parent communication at both primary and secondary level.

Progress and continuity

The National Curriculum is an important means of improving the links between primary and secondary schools. Despite the existence of many well-organized liaison schemes, there has been much concern about the problems of transfer from primary to secondary schools. Secondary teachers receiving pupils from different primary schools have found it difficult to establish the subject-content previously covered, or the level of attainment reached by individual children. It has not been unusual for secondary teachers to talk about 'starting from scratch'. This was particularly problematic in subjects where knowledge tends to build up sequentially, for example, in mathematics, science, and perhaps music. A research study from the University of Leicester showed children actually falling back in attainment when moving schools. The National Curriculum provides a focus for better record-keeping and monitoring of progress between teachers and between schools.

All these arguments apply equally where forms of schooling other than primary and secondary exist. In some areas the existence of middle schools, or junior high schools, means that children have two changes of school, rather than the more usual one. Many families have to move from place to place because of job opportunities. Even within the same school, teachers move to new posts, fall ill, or are involved in in-service training. These events can lead to significant breaks in the continuity of children's education. Again, the National Curriculum is a means of minimizing disruption.

Individual attainment

Finally, there is one major potential advantage of the National Curriculum that could radically change the way school-days are experienced. Many parents will remember the monthly or termly 'position in class' lists compiled by form teachers. Similar lists were drawn up to describe the end-of-term examination results. Grading schemes might also have been used; in many schools A–E for attainment and 1–5 for effort were widely adopted in the 1970s and 1980s. Most of these schemes involved ranking pupils one against another, and in fact throughout the twentieth century this has been the major form of assessment in British schools. Inevitably, a large proportion of pupils came out as below average.

Rank order is most significant when it determines access to limited places, for example, at universities or the administrative grades of the Civil Service. The public examination system served this purpose for most of this century. The 11-plus examination, which selected about 20 per cent of the age group to go on to a grammar school education, is one of the best-known examples of rank ordering. The statistical model upon which the tests and examinations were based was the bell curve, with the bulk of the population (average performance) found at the top of the curve, and the most or least able on the extremities (see Fig. 1).

Many of those who have advocated a National Curriculum argue

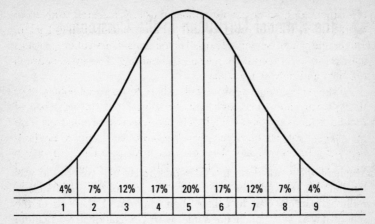

4%	7%	12%	17%	20%	17%	12%	7%	4%
1	2	3	4	5	6	7	8	9

Fig. 1   Bell curve chart

that we should be moving away from standards based on relative information (how one pupil compares with others) to absolute standards (whether a pupil has shown individual knowledge and competency in the different parts of the curriculum). Everyone should be able to achieve the higher levels of attainment, it is argued. A government-appointed Task Group on Assessment and Performance, set up to work out how the National Curriculum should be assessed, said that any system should be confined to 'the assessment of "performance" or "attainment"', and they were not recommending any attempt to assess separately the problematic notion of underlying 'ability'.

This represents something of a challenge of school organizations where ranking still lives on. For the most part the 'position in class' lists have disappeared, but in teachers' and parents' minds the old idea, discredited by many of the developments in psychology, that children are born with a fixed potential, remains. The National Curriculum provides a national yardstick against which unrecognized potential can be realized and acknowledged.

3 The National Curriculum in the Classroom

Much of the work done in classrooms today will reflect the way teaching has evolved over many years. The look of the primary classroom as parents wait to collect their children at the end of the school day is very much the same as in pre-National Curriculum days, with children putting away books and pens, clearing up art materials, or perhaps tidying the reading-corner. The teacher might be asking two children to tell the rest of the class tomorrow morning about the plants they are growing in the school garden. In secondary schools, pupils will almost certainly have spent the day moving from one specialist area to another. Homework will have been set in certain subjects. Some classes may have been asked to interview their parents about 'school-day memories' as part of a project in English. In many schools such a project will involve links with the history department. Sometimes there will have been class-centred lessons, with a teacher introducing a part of the scheme of work or syllabus and the pupils following this up with individual exercises or note-taking. In other classes, design tasks in technology, experiments in science, or a problem-solving exercise in mathematics may have involved pupils working together in groups of three or four.

In the next two sections examples show the National Curriculum at work in the classroom.

Planning the curriculum in the primary school

One major outcome of the introduction of the National Curriculum in the primary school has been an increase in whole school curriculum planning. The need to teach the content of the nine foundation subjects and RE to the level of detail required in the initial statutory orders would place a very heavy burden on the class teacher if left to a lone teacher and squeezed into the weekly timetable, especially at Key Stage 2. Most schools set up working groups led by the different subject curriculum leaders to analyse the requirements of the different subject orders at the different levels, and to draw up outline curriculum plans for Key Stage 1 and Key Stage 2. In this way the staff were able to pick out areas of 'overlap' between different subject areas, making the content rather more manageable.

At the same time, schools were being encouraged to reappraise the common practice of primary planning in terms of integrated topics (sometimes called 'themes' or 'projects' or 'centres of interest'). Some examples of the sort of primary topics that were common are 'Ourselves', 'Transport', 'Flight', 'Homes'. Other teachers chose more general concepts as a central focus, such as 'Growth and Change' or 'Movement'.

The strength of planning within topics is that the learning that is offered to children is not fragmented into different subjects and presented in different slots in the children's day. A well-planned integrated curriculum allows children to follow an area up in depth, drawing on their own experience, and to explore the links between the different subjects. However, not all integrated curriculum planning was successful. There was some concern noted by HMI, in the 1992 DES report on the primary curriculum, for example, that topic work was sometimes undemanding, lacking in progression, and at worst amounted to little more than copying from books.

Whole school curriculum planning, then, had to analyse the National Curriculum requirements for each subject and use these to redesign the curriculum to give breadth, balance, and continuity across the Key Stages, addressing criticisms such as those above. Topics, for example, began to be planned over a two-year cycle, with a different topic for each half-term. Each topic now tended to have a particular subject bias, so that teachers could ensure children worked on each of the foundation subject areas over a two-year cycle. An example over two terms from one school quoted in *Eating the Elephant Bit by Bit: The National Curriculum at Key Stage 2* (Webb 1993) shows how the following topics were linked to subjects:

Autumn: Transport (science and geography);
           Story-telling (English and technology).

Spring: Invaders (history and English);
           Healthy Living (science and geography).

If in one year topics focused on one subject more than others, the balance would be redressed in the next year.

Alongside plans for topic-related work, schools also often drew up plans for ongoing units of work across subjects, such as the school's mathematics scheme, music lessons with a specialist, and 'quiet reading' sessions. Within English they also planned subject-focused 'mini-topics', to run parallel with the main class topic, covering subject-focused work that it was not easy to integrate into the class topics, or special events such as a school Book Week or preparation for the Chinese New Year. Although topic-based planning remained very strong in primary schools, after the introduction of the National Curriculum teachers reported a move towards planning topics around subjects and a more widespread recognition that one integrated topic could not carry the whole curriculum, but that more than one form of planning was needed at any time.

Let us give an example of what a half-term topic might look like in practice in the Key Stage 1 classroom. In this example, our class teacher, who had a first degree in mathematics, planned his work within the frame of a whole school curriculum, drawing on the advice and support of the other curriculum subject specialists in the school. This half-term his main topic focus was the theme 'Growth and Change'. Having looked through the subject orders for his main focus, English, and his subsidiary focus, science (for this term), he drew up an outline of areas of the programme of study which he intended to focus on. He adapted his plans so that the starting-point reflected some of the current interests of the children in his class. One of them had talked about her new baby brother as the children sat in a circle on the carpet, sharing news. The other children had shown a lot of interest and had shared their own experience of babies. Some of them had gone on to write about babies they knew, drawing pictures and using a simple programme on the computer to write captions.

The teacher knew an older child in the school whose mother had just had a new baby. The mother agreed to bring the baby into the class regularly for a couple of months, so the children could see it growing and then record some of the ways in which it was changing. After watching the baby being weighed, and helping to log the results on a wall chart, the children asked the mother questions. She told them about the baby clinic she visited, and the children were fascinated. The teacher decided to turn the 'home corner' into a baby clinic. To structure their play he provided plenty of dolls, a variety of weighing scales, a 'changing table', and a baby bath. He also provided pencils and notepads for the children to fill in their baby's records, and kept an 'appointments book' next to an old telephone for writing down 'appointments' (encouraging emergent writing).

The following week he was able to arrange for a small group to visit the baby clinic and report back to the class. Two bilingual children in the class were able to report that they had interviewed a doctor at the clinic who turned out to share their languages, and, working together with the help of a bilingual support teacher, they developed an account of the conversation in English and Bengali on the class word-processor.

As the topic progressed, the teacher developed the theme to cover other subjects. In science, for example, the science programme of study under the heading 'Life Processes and Living Things' requires all children to be taught about how humans need food and water to stay alive, and that humans can produce babies and these babies grow into children and then adults. Children at this age are expected to relate simple scientific ideas to the evidence that exists for them. The topic provided plenty of opportunities for the teacher to develop work in these areas. It was also linked to mathematics, where the programme of study expects children to be able to collect, record, and interpret data using a range of charts, diagrams, tables, and graphs. As part of the history curriculum the children and the teacher brought in photographs of themselves as babies, and produced their own 'time-lines' showing some of the changes that had happened to them from birth to 5 years old.

Indeed, the teacher found the problem was not finding ways to extend the topic out into different curriculum areas, but where to stop. He could, for example, have made a map of the route the class went on to visit the local baby clinic, bringing in geography as well. Teachers have continually to make decisions about how wide-ranging or restricted their topics should be, depending on their objectives at that time. The National Curriculum has been seen as offering help here. Here is the view of one headteacher:

Before, you didn't plan in the same detail as we plan now. I'm much more conscious of getting the balance between subjects . . . The problem with topics is that you have to decide what to leave out—perhaps we weren't selective enough before . . . that's why planning is so important, to have in your mind the areas of the curriculum that you want to cover and not to get side-tracked.

Equally, not every aspect of the primary curriculum is covered by the National Curriculum subjects, and, through this topic, the teacher was able to pick up an important cross-curricular theme, health and safety. At the same time, he did not try to squeeze the whole curriculum into the topic. The whole school plan allowed him to make choices in the confidence that areas not covered this term would be picked up in the future.

However, he did add a self-contained unit of work around technology which was unconnected to the topic, as he wanted to provide experiences of using particular construction materials with one small group at a time to build up their skills in preparation for the next term's topic. He also planned a mini-topic over one week to follow up a poem the children had heard in assembly, bringing in dance and music. Teachers need to maintain enough flexibility in their plans to respond to their pupils' particular skills and needs, and to the unforeseen events that happen around them.

At secondary level the same approach to planning is developed, although the starting-point is more likely to be through subjects.

Volcanoes and earthquakes: a secondary science project

Many people will remember studying volcanoes at school. It may have been in a science, geography, or even history lesson. Drawing a cross-section of an active volcano and hearing accounts of famous eruptions such as Krakatoa seem to stay long in most people's minds. The programme of study at Key Stage 3 requires pupils to know about geological change and the origins of different types of rock.

The teacher has planned a series of lessons around the topic. The children begin by reading an account of the San Francisco earthquake of 1906, and the more recent one in 1989. They then use a slide sequence that describes the eruption of Vesuvius. This provides the starting-point for a run of activities planned around a chapter in the textbook that looks at volcanoes and earthquakes and brings in other science curriculum issues. For example, pupils learn about the Richter Scale for measuring the intensity of an earthquake.

Schools plan the National Curriculum to maximize the cross-references that can be made to other subjects. The science teacher, for example, would be aware of English and mathematics attainment targets at level 5. The description of volcanic eruptions and earthquakes would develop English skills. Skills of data interpretation would be developed by looking at seismic graphs. The final part of this series of lessons is jointly taught by the class teachers of science and technology. The technology teacher has acquired a video that shows how high-rise buildings in places like San Francisco and Tokyo are constructed to withstand earth tremors and earthquakes.

4 Testing and Assessment

Testing and assessment is the issue that provokes the greatest controversy amongst educationists, parents, and the public generally. For pupils it can be one of the most worrying aspects of school life. It is also ultimately one of the most important. Tests, assessments, and examinations are a significant factor in determining job prospects or access to college or higher education. If you want to be a vet, the very highest grades at Advanced (A) Level will be required. No one can become a teacher without obtaining General Certificates of Secondary Education (GCSE) in English and mathematics at grades A to C. A levels are also required.

The National Curriculum is accompanied by national assessments. Previously, most pupils, apart from taking reading-tests, were well into secondary schooling before they came into contact with a nationally standardized examination. Now a measurement is being made from the age of 7 about the progress that has been achieved. Many parents support this idea. This is not surprising, as most people expect some sort of feedback about how well their children are doing.

Immediately, however, problems begin to arise. Testing children to see how much they know appears to many people a straightforward process. In Chapter 2 the difficulty of monitoring standards was explained. Producing fair and reliable ways of testing children is equally difficult, and the government has spent millions of pounds on research projects in attempting to solve the problems.

Assessment is full of jargon, and before explaining the issues and methods being used we need to define some of it. First, is there any difference between the terms 'tests', 'assessment', and 'examinations'? In practice the answer is no. All three terms are used interchangeably. Distinctions have begun to emerge, however, and in talking to teachers signs of this may be detected. Tests can describe short, usually written, assessments set and marked by teachers to see how well a group or class have learned in a particular topic. These help teachers in planning future work and activities for individuals and for classes as a whole. There are also now, however, national tests taken at the ages 7, 11, and 14 in the core subjects of English, mathematics, and science. These provide information on overall achievement in these subjects at the end of a Key Stage. Examinations tend now to refer to public examinations such as GCSE or A level, although some schools, almost wholly at the secondary level have end-of-year internal examinations for some or all of the year groups not taking public examinations. The term 'assessment', however, covers tests, examinations, and all the other ways in which teachers check and monitor progress.

The new approach to assessment

The sort of assessment the merely gives you a grade (like a formal public examination) tells you very little about which parts of the syllabus you did well on or where you went wrong. Giving you a position in a class list is much the same: all you can tell from the list is how you compare with others. The new approach to assessment attempts to do four things. First, it attempts to recognize when children have achieved a target, to acknowledge this in a positive way, and then to help them plan the next stages of learning. This is called *formative* assessment. Secondly, the assessment process aims to reveal weaknesses or difficulties in such a way that appropriate help can be given and the child can overcome the problem. This is termed the *diagnostic* purpose of assessment. This reflects the way most people learn. Initially learners experience patchy understanding. It is necessary to spot the areas of weakness and remedy them through extra work and attention. The driving-test, for example, tries to be diagnostic in that you are given feedback on the specific parts of the test you fail. As you trek back sadly to your friendly instructor for further lessons, it would serve little purpose merely to announce that you had a D fail grade! The detailed recording and judgements involved in teachers' continuous assessment should, if working well, provide important formative and diagnostic information for every child. It is worth emphasizing that the aim is *to show the child what he or she has achieved*, not where they have failed.

Thirdly, the assessment process aims to give teachers, the child, and parents an overall summary of what has been achieved, at regular intervals. This is termed the *summative* purpose of assessment. In the National Curriculum the summary is made on the basis of progress through the eight levels in the attainment targets of the different subjects up to age 14. This is discussed in greater detail later in the chapter. Fourthly, the results of these assessments are used by teachers, headteachers, and governors to see how well they are doing against the targets they will have established for the school as a whole. This could be called the *evaluative* purpose of assessment.

The results of national tests and public examinations are now recorded for each school and published. There has been much criticism of this. Schools situated in socially and economically advantaged areas almost always achieve better results than schools in an urban, deprived environment. To counter this a number of ways of showing the progress pupils make within a school, rather than just the outcome of tests and examinations, are being developed to place alongside the results of tests and examinations. This is an important aspect of the evaluative use to which assessment can be put.

In the examples of classroom activities in Chapter 3 you will have seen how the teacher can use assessment for formative and diagnostic purposes. This is, of course, nothing new. The best teachers have always used a similar approach. The National Curriculum has given an added impetus to this, and in particular, the chance to make assessment a positive experience for the child. Two further phrases help explain this more clearly.

The old system of assessment was almost wholly *norm referenced*, that is, pupils were placed in rank order and predetermined proportions were placed in the various grades. It implies that grades are assigned by comparison to other pupils' performance, rather than by the quality of the individual's performance. The idea of predetermined proportions was considered in Chapter 2. The 'bell curve' was, and in some examinations still is, used to allocate grades. The great difficulty with norm referencing is that a proportion of pupils are inevitably deemed to have done badly, and come away with a negative experience not only of the examination or test but of school generally.

The alternative to norm referencing is termed *criterion refer-encing*, and it is this that the National Curriculum assessments attempt to achieve. By this is meant a system where a pupil's achieve-ments are judged in relation to specific objectives, irrespective of other pupils' performance. As we have seen, if the pupil shows com-petency against different descriptions of levels of attainment, then he or she will be deemed to have achieved success. The driving-test is often used as an example of criterion referencing. Success or failure depends on a display of competency against specified criteria.

Categories of assessment

First, there is *continuous assessment* (also known as teacher assess-ment) by the teacher or teachers. This is the daily and weekly record in all aspects of the curriculum organized by the teacher and trans-ferred on to individual records. Every so often the teacher will look at the detailed records of progress and make a judgement about the level of work being achieved by the child.

Secondly there are *national tests*. These are written and set out-side the school by organizations commissioned by SCAA. Towards the end of a key stage children will complete a number of activ-ities that will be marked and recorded to measure their level of attainment in a limited number of subjects (English, mathematics, and science). These tests will serve two purposes: first, in combi-nation with the teacher assessments they will be used to report to parents and others the levels the children have reached in particu-lar subjects at the end of each key stage. Secondly, by comparing the levels reached by children on these national tests with the judge-ment being made by teachers through the continuous assessment process, it will be possible to check that teacher assessments are in line with nationally agreed standards. More information on tests is given in the next section.

Teachers use all sorts of ways of *recording assessment continu-ously*. They will take information from written work, from children's answers to questions, and from the way the children perform prac-tical tasks individually or in a group.

The nature of the assessment tasks, their purpose in the assess-ment of children, and the relationship between teacher assessment and national tests have been the subject of intense debate. A review completed at the end of 1993 and upon which the revised National Curriculum introduced in 1995 was based made it very clear that the task of assessing the National Curriculum had become too bureaucratic. The report was particularly insistent that teachers need not keep elaborate tick lists for every attainment target at every level:

Records supplement the teacher's personal and professional knowledge of a child. It is not possible for teachers to record all their knowledge and they should not be tempted to try. Written records complement this professional understanding. If record systems do not provide a significant contribution to teaching and learning there is little point in maintaining them (Dearing 1993: 102).

Records of children's attainments are likely to contain details that will inform reports to parents. Records that are over-detailed or complex tend to hinder rather than support this task. They should help identify clearly the child's strengths, weaknesses and progress for parents and provide information that will indicate the next steps forward for the child (Dearing 1993: 103).

And a year later in 1994, when the government had accepted all the proposed revisions, the chairman of SCAA and the chief inspector of schools reiterated this message in a letter that went to all schools:

we are looking to teachers to make a rounded judgement on which description best fits the overall performance of the individual child. There is no question of looking for an exact fit. Children may well be more advanced in one aspect of a subject than another, and it is, therefore, very much a matter for the teacher to decide which description best matches their overall performance.

Teachers will naturally want to keep some evidence for the basis of their judgements. But even in English, mathematics and science, where teacher assessment is statutory at the end of key stage, there is no need for the detailed records kept by many schools in relation to statements of attainment.

How continuous assessment works

Teachers are unable to assess all the children in their class all the time. Throughout the year, therefore, it is likely that they will give particular attention to two or three children at a time. In the last section we saw some primary teaching focusing initially on English. The teacher could on one day:

- have individual conversations with four or five children to see if they could briefly describe an event from the previous day. The teacher will be experienced in judging whether the child is confident in doing this or whether further practice is needed (in which case the teacher may suggest an activity in the group where the child can practice further). The teacher would also make a mental (or perhaps written) note to have another conversation later in the week in which an event can be described briefly.

- after school, spend some time looking at the written work completed by all the children. The teacher would be looking, for example, for evidence of sentences with evidence of consistent use of capital letters, full stops, and question-marks. As she looked at the books the teacher would make a note against each child's record. It is unlikely that a judgement would be made about whether the child would be fully competent on the basis of one piece of written work. The teacher will have built up a knowledge of each child over the year and will use a variety of evidence in making a final teacher assessment.

The secondary science teacher working on rocks and soil will be involved in a similar process.

- In this class the teacher is using a recording system that allows her to note when pupils are successful with practical activities. In science classes today there are few occasions on which all children are asked to do the same activity, then stop and wait to have their work marked by the teacher. More commonly they carry out investigations and the teacher observes different parts of the process to see how well they are doing. During one week's lessons, therefore, the teacher may observe all the groups and make judgements about pupils' progress.

- In the same class the teacher may set a written assignment, following reading and discussion in class, that provides evidence of the child's understanding of different weathering processes that lead to different soil types. The teacher's written comments in the children's exercise books would indicate how well they had done and how, if necessary, they could go over the work again (or follow it up in a different way) to achieve a fresh understanding of the concept. Depending on how well the group as a whole had done, the teacher could decide: (1) to do something with the whole class on this, (2) to follow up the concept with a group of pupils, or (3) to give some individual help as the vast majority had clearly grasped what was involved.

Every so often teachers will take their records and make judgements about the level being achieved in each of the attainment targets they are covering in that subject. This is the information used to produce the annual report to parents, which includes details on teacher assessment results and national test results (in the final year of a key stage), as well as all the other information about how hard their child is working, whether he or she seems to be enjoying the subject, how regularly homework is being completed, attendance, and so forth. The right to receive an annual report on their child's progress and the opportunity to discuss it with a teacher is set out in the Parent's Charter and subsequent legislation on assessment, recording, and reporting. Parents may also wish to ask about the sort of recording system being used daily. Schools will be explaining this at parents' evenings or at special events to describe the way the National Curriculum works in practice. Each school has established its own record scheme, following advice from national organizations like SCAA, as well as from local advisers or inspectors.

The national tests

This was an area of major national controversy when the National Curriculum was first produced. Teachers complained that the tests were too time-consuming and disrupted the normal curriculum. Teachers and parents were worried about the fairness of the actual tests used. And everyone was concerned about the reporting of these tests in league-table format that provided a pecking-order of schools.

The major revision of the National Curriculum introduced in September 1995 brought about major changes in the organization and structure of national tests. The tests were substantially slimmed down and the role and standing of the teacher's assessment was given greater importance. Teacher assessment and national test results are now given equal standing. There may be variations between them because the simplified national tests cannot cover everything that teacher assessment does. Both results have to be interpreted and it is the responsibility of schools and teachers to ensure that parents have the opportunities to hear about the results and understand what they mean. This is an area where some modifications are likely, and it is important to consult with schools on the latest versions. Below is a key stage summary of what requirements there are for national tests.

Key Stage 1

There are national tests in English and mathematics. In English pupils are assessed in reading, writing, spelling, and handwriting. There are further individual reading tasks for pupils who have achieved level 2 (the average for the key stage). Pupils who do well on that test can take the further reading comprehension test to see if they have achieved level 3. In mathematics there is one test in number. Teachers must also assess children in science where there are are no national tests. Statutory teacher assessments in non-core subjects are to be reviewed once curriculum orders are in place.

Key Stage 2

There are two tests in English: assessing reading and writing. There is one test in mathematics and science and the final maths level will be for the subject overall, not for the separate attainment targets. Some opportunities in the testing will be given for pupils who are behind the majority of the class and for those who are ahead. Statutory teacher assessments in non-core subjects are to be reviewed once curriculum orders are in place.

Key Stage 3

National tests are only set in English, mathematics, and science. The tests are longer than at Key Stage 2—but not exceeding seven hours in all across the three subjects. Again there will be different activities for those behind or ahead of the majority of the class. There are two papers in English (one of which covers one of the compulsory Shakespeare plays that have been studied) and two in each of the other subjects.

Teachers must also give parents information on teacher assessments that cover the non-core subjects once the revised National Curriculum orders are in place.

To avoid overloading teachers, the tests at Key Stage 3 are being marked by external assessors. This has led to some controversy about accuracy, particularly in English, and represents another case that will be under review! Examples of questions set within the national tests are given under the subjects described in the chapters that follow.

These tests and the legal necessity to report to parents in other subjects only represent one part of the curriculum, although it is a central and important part. In considering the assessment of any pupil it is important to look at the children's achievements across the whole curriculum. This is recognized nationally in the development over the last decade of records of achievement for all pupils.

Records of achievement

Alongside teachers' continuous assessment, national tests, and public examinations, there has been another development that has had an impact on a great many schools. *Records of achievement* were first planned in the 1970s and early 1980s, to give much greater acknowledgement to what young people achieved in school. Originally this began in secondary schools, where the vast majority of school leavers had very little to show for their efforts and enthusiasm across the broad range of school life. Examination results gave an indication of academic attainment, but what about all the other qualities that schools have a responsibility to develop?

Achievements in creative activities, the school play or other aspects of drama, music, and dance, gained little recognition. Sporting achievement may have gained passing recognition, but there was no ongoing record that the pupils could take away with them. And then there are the host of other pursuits that the good school fosters: outdoor activities, community help programmes, and charity fundraising, to give just three examples. Only in a very few schools had these been systematically recorded.

By the late 1980s a great many schools were using a 'record of achievement'. The form and style varied from area to area, but most aimed to record achievements in all aspects of school life. Some also recorded important achievements outside school. Now all children will leave school with a National Record of Achievement. The pupil usually works with a form teacher or counsellor to compile and collate the records. These contain information about academic work as well, including grades obtained in examinations. Achievements on the way to public examinations are as important as the final grades, and nearly all records of achievement recognize this. Many young people choose to use their record at interviews with potential employers or when transferring to other forms of education. It is also a document to be kept at home, treasured, and years later shown with some pride to the grandchildren!

The future

The public and political controversies that were associated with testing in the early 1990s have now given way to a degree of consensus. Teachers accept that parents want some measure of individual, school, and national progress. Government has accepted that it is hugely time-consuming to try and test in every subject at every key stage. Teachers' continuous assessments, made against the *level descriptions* of the National Curriculum must, however, be explained to parents who now have a statutory right for information on how their children are progressing. National tests, after some early expensive failures, have now been developed in a more simplified form. Attempts to make these more fair and accurate will continue. The most likely area for development in the second half of the 1990s and through into the new millennium is in the area of A levels and the range of new vocational qualifications that have been developed for the increasing numbers staying on in full-time education after the age of 16. This is a complex area about which schools and colleges can provide more detailed information.

Testing and assessment in Northern Ireland

The education system in Northern Ireland is similar in many respects to those in England and Wales, though differences do exist in respect of both the style and substance of its curriculum, assessment, and examination arrangements.

As in England and Wales, most pupils enter for GCSE examinations and a significant number stay on at school to follow GCE A-Level courses. Since 1994 all pupils have left school with a National Record of Achievement, while an increasing number appear likely in future years to gain vocational qualifications such as GNVQs. However, a significant difference to elsewhere in the United Kingdom is the retention of a selective system of secondary education in most parts of the Province.

Like the National Curriculum, the Northern Ireland Curriculum, introduced in 1989, aimed to guarantee all pupils a broad and balanced education throughout the years of compulsory schooling. Programmes of study were developed for a large number of individual subjects, each including attainment targets and statements of attainment to enable pupil progress across four key stages to be measured against a ten-level scale of attainment and be reported to parents at the end of each key stage. Also like the National Curriculum, the Northern Ireland Curriculum has been subject to a major review exercise, and revised curriculum requirements will apply from September 1996. Unlike the National Curriculum, however, the curricular framework in Northern Ireland has grouped cognate subjects under six main areas of study headings (English, Mathematics, Science and Technology, Environment and Society, Creative and Expressive Studies, and Language Studies) and identified six cross-curricular or educational themes related to the specific needs of young people in the Province, which from the outset were built into the programmes of study of individual subjects. These unique elements, together with the assessment arrangements which have evolved in Northern Ireland, have helped make the educational experiences of its pupils distinct from those elsewhere.

Pilot assessment arrangements were introduced at Key Stages 2 and 3 in the 1992/3 school year and at Key Stage 1 in 1993/4. In Northern Ireland Key Stage 1 covers Years 1–4; Key Stage 2, Years 5–7; Key Stage 3, Years 8–10; and Key Stage 4, Years 11–12.

The assessment arrangements applied to English and Mathematics at Key Stages 1 and 2, and English, Mathematics, and Science at Key Stage 3. The common features of the 1992/3 arrangements at both Key Stages 2 and 3 were that:

- the assessment outcomes of pupils should be arrived at ~~by~~ combining the teachers' assessments with the results of externally set formal tests called common assessment instruments (CAIs);
- teachers would be helped to assess their pupils through the introduction of external assessment resources (EARs) which were designed to act as formative and diagnostic assessment tools and be used as normal classroom activities;
- a system of individual pupil moderation would be set in place as a quality-control mechanism to ensure a consistency of standards within and across all schools.

In response to the views expressed by teachers concerning the appropriateness, manageability, and usefulness of the pilot arrangements significant changes were made to them during 1994 and 1995. For example:

- CAIs and EARs were replaced by a range of shorter, externally devised assessment units (AUs);
- the aim of AUs is to confirm teacher assessment, and they permit assessment to be carried out in schools in a more flexible and less intrusive manner than CAIs. The pilot assessments require the use of a number of units in the last two terms of a key stage, but otherwise teachers can choose which units they want to use and when to use them;
- the requirement to assess pupils against individual statements of attainment was removed and replaced by the collective use of statements of attainment to aid teachers to make more holistic judgements than previously;
- individual pupil moderation was replaced by a quality assurance moderation system which significantly reduced the demands on teachers associated with the selection and collection of evidence and placed the emphasis upon in-service training of teachers.

In March 1995 the Northern Ireland education minister, Michael Ancram, announced that he proposed to discontinue the pilot assessment arrangements and introduce statutory assessment arrangements in the 1996/7 school year at Key Stages 1, 2, and 3, when teachers would also be commencing teaching the revised curriculum. The aim of the revision was to slim down the curriculum and make it more appropriate for pupils and manageable for teachers. Major proposals arising out of the revision exercise are:

- a reduction in the statutory curriculum time at all key stages;
- reduced programme of study content in many subjects;
- the replacement of statements of attainment by level descriptions, which are general descriptions of pupils' performance and are intended to be used by teachers to confirm their professional judgement about pupils' attainment at the end of Key Stages 1, 2, and 3;
- full programmes of study only for compulsory subjects at Key Stage 4, with other subjects being specified through outline programmes of study. (As in England and Wales, a decision has already been taken not to apply the ten-level scale of attainment at Key Stage 4);
- to take account of the interests of those pupils who have special educational needs, all programmes of study at Key Stages 1, 2, and 3 will start at Level 1.

Programmes of study will cover:

Levels 1–3 at Key Stage 1
Levels 1–5 at Key Stage 2
Levels 1–8 at Key Stage 3

effectively making it an eight- rather than a ten-level scale of attainment.

When making his announcement about the introduction of statutory assessment the minister promised teachers that he would not be making any decisions on the form it should take until he had heard their views via a full consultation exercise to be carried out by the Northern Ireland Council for the Curriculum, Examinations, and Assessment (CCEA). He did, however, consider that there were three basic options available:

- a teacher assessment model similar to that employed in the pilot years;
- a tests-only model;
- a format including both teacher assessment and external tests.

He also added that teachers should consider each of the three options in light of the issues of:

- the publication of results;
- the transfer system at Key Stage 2;
- which subjects should be formally assessed at Key Stage 3.

5 The Core Foundation Subjects: English, Mathematics, and Science

English

The working group that devised the first National Curriculum order for English structured its thinking around five models of English: the influence of these models is still clearly discernible in the final English programmes of study, with a stronger emphasis placed on some views than on others:

1   a 'personal growth' view focuses on the child: it emphasizes the relationship between language and learning in the individual child, and the role of literature in developing children's imaginative and aesthetic lives;

2   a 'cross-curricular' view focuses on the school: it emphasizes that all teachers have a responsibility to help children with the language demands of different subjects on the school curriculum. In England, English is different from other school subjects in that it is both a subject and a medium of instruction for other subjects;

3   an 'adult-needs' view focuses on communication outside the school: it emphasizes the responsibility of English teachers to prepare children for the language demands of adult life, including the workplace, in a fast-changing world. Children need to learn to deal with day-to-day demands of spoken language and of print; they also need to be able to write clearly, appropriately, and effectively;

4   a 'cultural heritage' view emphasizes the responsibility of schools to lead children to an appreciation of those works of

literature that have been widely regraded as amongst the finest in the language;

5 a 'cultural analysis' view emphasizes the role of English in helping children towards a critical understanding of the world and cultural environment in which they live. Children should know about the processes by which meanings are conveyed, and about the ways in which print and other media carry values.

Although no explicit reference is made to these models in the final English programmes of study and attainment targets, they provide an important and interesting background to the debates out of which this English curriculum has emerged.

Programmes of Study

The Programmes of Study provide the basis for planning and teaching the English curriculum. They are organized into three main areas:

> Speaking and Listening;
> Reading;
> and Writing.

Whilst these areas are separated into different sections, it is emphasized that 'pupils' abilities should be developed within an *integrated programme* of speaking and listening, reading and writing'. So, for example, whilst an English teacher may choose to highlight reading in a sequence of lessons, pupils will inevitably be involved in speaking, listening, and writing tasks as well.

English, unlike other subjects, sets out General Requirements for teaching the subject across all the key stages. This is an important statement and is set out in full below:

1. English should develop pupils' abilities to communicate effectively in speech and writing and to listen with understanding. It should also enable them to be enthusiastic, responsive and knowledgeable readers.

a To develop effective speaking and listening pupils should be taught to:
   • use the vocabulary and grammar of standard English;
   • formulate, clarify and express their ideas;

- adapt their speech to a widening range of circumstances and demands;
- listen, understand and respond appropriately to others.

b To develop as effective readers, pupils should be taught to:
- read accurately, fluently and with understanding;
- understand and respond to the texts they read;
- read, analyse and evaluate a wide range of texts, including literature from the English literary heritage and from other cultures and traditions.

c To develop as effective writers, pupils should be taught to use:
- compositional skills—developing ideas and communicating meaning to a reader, using a wide-ranging vocabulary and an effective style, organising and structuring sentences grammatically and whole texts coherently;
- presentational skills—accurate punctuation, correct spelling and legible handwriting;
- a widening variety of forms for different purposes.

2. In order to participate confidently in public, cultural and working life, pupils need to be able to speak, write and read standard English fluently and accurately. All pupils are therefore entitled to the full range of opportunities necessary to enable them to develop competence in standard English. The richness of dialects and other languages can make an important contribution to pupils' knowledge and understanding of standard English. Where appropriate, pupils should be encouraged to make use of their understanding and skills in other languages when learning English.

3. In Wales, the linguistic and cultural knowledge of Welsh-speaking pupils should be recognised and used when developing their competence in English. Teaching should ensure that such pupils are given access to the full scope of the programmes of study . . .

4. Pupils should be given opportunities to develop their understanding and use of standard English and to recognise that:
- standard English is distinguished from other forms of English by its vocabulary, and by rules and conventions of grammar, spelling and punctuation;
- the grammatical features that distinguish standard English include how pronouns, adverbs and adjectives should be used and how negatives, questions and verb tenses should be formed; such features are present in both the spoken and written forms, except where non-standard forms are used for effect or technical reasons;
- differences between the spoken and written forms relate to

the spontaneity of speech and to its function in conversation, whereas writing is more permanent, often carefully crafted, and less dependent on immediate responses;

- spoken standard English is not the same as Received Pronunciation and can be expressed in a variety of accents.

The Programmes of Study are then set out in more detail for each key stage in the three areas of Speaking and Listening, Reading, and Writing. These in turn are divided into three separate sections:

> Range
> Key Skills
> Standard English and Language Study

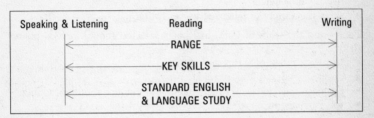

For example, at Key Stage 2 under the *Range* section for *Reading* it is required that:

Pupils' reading should include texts:
- with challenging subject matter that broadens perspectives and extends thinking;
- with more complex narrative structures and sustained ideas;
- that include figurative language, both in poetry and prose;
- with a variety of structural and organisational features.

The literature read should cover the following categories:

- a range of modern fiction by significant children's authors;
- some long-established children's fiction;
- a range of good quality modern poetry;
- some classic poetry;
- texts drawn from a variety of cultures and traditions;
- myths, legends and traditional stories.

At Key Stages 3 and 4 the programme of study for reading under the *Range* section includes the following:

The literature read should be drawn from a variety of genres, including plays, novels, short stories and poetry.

Plays selected should include works that:
- extend pupils' understanding of drama in performance, *e.g. direction, portrayal and interpretation of character;*
- show variety in the structure, *e.g. tragedy, comedy, farce,* and *setting;*
- extend pupils' ideas and their moral and emotional understanding;
- use language in rich, diverse ways.

Novels and short stories selected should include works that:
- include a range of narrative structures and literary techniques;
- extend pupils' ideas and their moral and emotional understanding;
- offer perspectives on society and community and their impact on the lives of individuals;
- show the variety of language use in fiction.

Poetry and the work of individual poets selected should include poems that:
- feature a range of forms and styles;
- draw on oral and literary traditions;
- extend pupils' ideas and their moral and emotional understanding;
- use language in imaginative, precise and original ways.

Pupils should read texts from other cultures and traditions that represent their distinctive voices and forms, and offer varied perspectives and subject matter.

Attainment targets

There are three attainment targets for English in the national curriculum:

AT1. Speaking and Listening
AT2. Reading
AT3. Writing

An extract from the attainment targets at Key Stage 1 in Speaking and Listening at level 1 requires that:

Pupils talk about matters of immediate interest. They listen to others and usually respond appropriately. They convey simple meanings to a range of listeners, speaking audibly, and begin to extend their ideas or accounts by providing some detail.

By the end of Key Stage 2 (7–11) at level 4:

Pupils talk and listen with confidence in an increasing range of contexts. Their talk is adapted to the purpose: developing ideas thoughtfully, describing events and conveying their opinions clearly. In discussion, they listen carefully, making contributions and asking questions that are responsive to others' ideas and views. They use appropriately some of the features of standard English vocabulary and grammar.

At the end of Key Stage 3 (11–14) at level 6:

Pupils adapt their talk to the demands of different contexts with increasing confidence. Their talk engages the interest of the listener through the variety of its vocabulary and expression. Pupils take an active part in discussion, showing understanding of ideas and sensitivity to others. They are usually fluent in their use of standard English in formal situations.

By Key Stage 4 (14–16) at level 7:

Pupils are confident in matching their talk to the demands of different contexts. They use vocabulary precisely and organize their talk to communicate clearly. In discussion, pupils make significant contributions, evaluating others' ideas and varying how and when they participate. They show confident use of standard English in situations that require it.

At the highest levels of attainment, where exceptional performance can be recorded:

Pupils select and use structures, styles and registers appropriately in a range of contexts, varying their vocabulary and expression confidently for a range of purposes. They initiate and sustain discussion through the sensitive use of a variety of contributions. They take a leading role in discussion and listen with concentration and understanding to varied and complex speech. They show assured and fluent use of standard English in a range of situations and for a variety of purposes.

We can see from these extracts that the National Curriculum attainment targets require an increasing complexity of skills from pupils as they progress through the levels. Yet one of the difficulties of describing progress in this way is the nature of learning: pupils rarely learn in such a neat, linear way. Rather, learning is recursive: there are times of great progress, followed by a period of consolidation, or even some falling back. However, whilst recognizing this, the level descriptors act as a guide to the features that English teachers should consider in recording a pupil's overall achievement at the end of a key stage. English teachers will use their knowledge of pupils' work across a range of contexts and from different times as well as exemplar material across a range of attainment in this process. They are also encouraged to 'consider the descriptions from adjacent levels to ensure that a rounded judgment is made' (SCAA 1994).

Standard English and Language Study

We have seen that Standard English and Language Study is a requirement across the key stages. The following extracts from the programmes of study for Key Stages 3 and 4 illustrate this aspect of the English Orders:

Speaking and listening

a Pupils should be taught to be fluent, accurate users of standard English vocabulary and grammar, and to recognise its importance as the language of public communication. They should be taught to adapt their talk to suit the circumstances, and to be confident users of standard English in formal and informal situations. In role-play and drama, the vocabulary, structures and tone appropriate to such contexts should be explored.

b Pupils should be given opportunities to consider the development of English, including:
  • how usage, words and meanings change over time;
  • how words and parts of words are borrowed from other languages;
  • the coinage of new words and the origins of existing words;
  • current influences on spoken and written language;
  • attitudes to language use;
  • the differences between speech and writing;
  • the vocabulary and grammar of standard English and dialectal variations.

Reading

a Pupils should be taught to recognise, analyse and evaluate the characteristic features of different types of text in print and other media. They should be given opportunities to consider the effects of organisation and structure, how authors' purposes and intentions are portrayed, and how attitudes, values and meanings are communicated.

b Pupils should be taught:
- about the main characteristics of literary language, including figures of speech and sound patterning;
- to consider features of the vocabulary and grammar of standard English that are found in different types of text, *e.g. technical terms in reports, rhetorical devices in speeches*;
- to analyse and evaluate the use of language in a variety of media, making comparisons where appropriate, *e.g. the treatment of a traditional story in a children's picture book and in its original source; a comparison of a television news bulletin with a report on the same event in a newspaper*;
- about different genres and their characteristics, including language, structure and organisational features;
- to analyse techniques, *e.g. the portrayal of setting and period, the weaving of parallel narratives, time shifts, the building of suspense, the use of imagery*.

Writing

a Pupils should be encouraged to be confident in the use of formal and informal written standard English, using the grammatical, lexical and orthographic features of standard English, except where non-standard forms are required for effect or technical reasons. They should be taught about variation in the written forms and how these differ from spoken forms and dialects. Pupils should be given a range of opportunities to use the syntax and vocabulary characteristic of English in formal writing, *e.g. business letter, critical review, informative article*, and to distinguish varying degrees of formality, selecting appropriately for a task. They should be encouraged to relate their study of language to their reading and their previous linguistic experience, written and oral.

b Pupils should be encouraged to broaden their understanding of the principles of sentence grammar and be taught to organise whole texts effectively. Pupils should be given opportunities to analyse their own writing, reflecting on the meaning and clarity of individual sentences, using appropriate terminology . . .

c Pupils should be encouraged to consider apt and imaginative choices of vocabulary and the precise use of words, including consideration of synonyms and double meanings. Pupils should be given opportunities to use dictionaries and thesauruses to explore derivations and alternative meanings.

This is an area of the English curriculum which generates some of the liveliest and intense debates in English, specifically concerning recommendations over Standard English and the teaching of grammar. *The Sun*, for example, made much of this in earlier debates.

Standard English can be defined as a dialect of English, with the understanding that dialect refers to grammar and vocabulary, but not to accent. That all pupils should learn, and if necessary be explicitly taught, Standard English is justified by reference to its widespread use in the education system and in professional life, in public and formal uses, and in writing and particularly in print. Since Standard English is the language of wider communication, its teaching becomes an issue of access. The controversy arises over the social prestige of Standard English (which is why it is often, but wrongly, confused with received pronunciation. Standard English can be spoken with any accent.) The extensive use of Standard English in public life has led to it often being seen as superior to non-standard, or regional, dialects. The difference between Standard English and other varieties of English actually lies in vocabulary and syntax. Creole varieties of English, for example, Black British English and Patois, are recognized as having their own complex and rule-governed structure. Standard English itself changes with time and use. It is for social and historical reasons that non-standard dialects have repeatedly and incorrectly been represented as simplified variations of Standard English.

Whilst the National Curriculum is clear that it is the entitlement of all pupils to learn Standard English, the aim must be to add Standard English to the repertoire of pupils, not to replace other dialects or languages. 'The richness of dialects and other languages can make an important contribution to pupils' knowledge and understanding of standard English. Where appropriate pupils should be encouraged to make use of their understanding and skills in other languages when learning English. In Wales the linguistic and cultural knowledge of Welsh-speaking pupils should be recognized and used when developing their competence in English.'

The teaching of grammar inspires the same level of debate. Grammar is often understood to mean the correct use of the standard language, and again much of the controversy stems from this fundamental misapprehension of the term 'grammar'. Linguists distinguish between prescriptive grammar (the view that it is possible

ERE! NOW KIDS DON'T 'AVE TO TALK PROPER

By ROBERT BOLTON

TEACHERS no longer need to correct the bad grammar of pupils, a new report on English claimed yesterday.

The top-level document, backed by Education Secretary Kenneth Baker, says teachers have 'little hope' of changing the way children speak.

It adds: 'There is little point in correcting the spoken language of pupils in any general way.'

But last night Tory MP Sir Rhodes Boyson slammed the report's conclusions.

He said: 'Teachers should be putting across proper English and expect to be spoken to in the same way by children.

'Grammar has to be taught. It is not something children are born with.'

Sir Rhodes, a former headmaster, added: 'Standard English is the pass-port to mobility.

'Sloppiness in speech rules you out for a job.

WOOLLY

'One of the reasons why we are so bad at foreign languages is because we don't know the grammar of our own language.'

The report, produced by a 10-strong committee, states that children should know when to use proper English.

It adds: 'They should recognise that "we was, he ain't, they never" are not grammatical.'

The report was 'beefed up' after Mr Baker complained that an earlier version was 'too woolly.'

It will be sent to head teachers, school governors and parents for their views.

Fig. 2 *Sun* Report

to lay down rules for the correct use of language), and descriptive grammar (the view that the way people actually use language should be accurately described, without prescription of how they ought to use it). Such views need not be seen as mutually exclusive; we need both accurate descriptions of language related to situations, purposes, and mode as well as prescriptions that take account of appropriateness in a given context. The National Curriculum for English recognizes both these views in its sections on Language Study, as will be clear from the extract below. Teaching grammar has not, then, been abandoned by English teachers; in fact, quite the opposite. The concept has been widened to look at how language works, and English teachers remain concerned to ensure that teaching about language is made relevant and immediate to their pupils.

The National Curriculum has certain qualifications for pupils who live in Wales. For example, in Welsh-speaking classes at Key Stage 1 pupils do not have to follow the Key Stage 1 National Curriculum in English.

A further area of controversy has been assessment in the methods used, the form that national tests have taken, and the fact that test results were given precedence over teacher assessment. The complete rewrite of the National Curriculum which took place in 1994 was in part due to the political pressure exerted by the very large numbers of English teachers who boycotted the first attempts to provide national tests. These tests were seen as simplistic and crude and failing to provide an accurate view of the pupils progress across the English curriculum as a whole. Many still hold to this view and the debate about what should be assessed in English, and how, will continue as long as national testing exists. Teacher assessment has now, however, been accorded equal status with end-of-key-stage tests and there has been some acceptance that some form of testing is demanded by parents. The boycotts have been dropped and attention has focused on trying to make the tests as fair as possible. The following are examples of tasks set for pupils in the Key Stages 1, 2, and 3 English tests.

The first extract is taken from the 1994 Standard Task for Writing (AT3) at Key Stage 1. Only 'Part A: Writing a Story' is shown. There are further sections (e.g. Redrafting, Spelling from Writing) that follow on from this task for pupils judged to have demonstrated evidence of attainment in level 3 or above in this writing task.

Part A: Writing a Story

* Children who may be assessed against the level 4 criteria should be encouraged to write a story suitable for level 4 assessment. It is not necessary to ask them to write a further story specifically for level 4.

SoA	Evidence of Attainment
Resources	You will need writing materials. En 3 *Pupil Sheet 1* can be used if you wish.
What to do	
• Help the children to decide on subjects and titles for their stories.	The children may suggest for whom the story is being written or you may set a particular stimulus, starting point or theme for the writing, there is no need to use the same one for the whole class.
• Help the children decide why they are writing their stories and who is to be their audience.	Not all children will produce their best work if they write for their friends in the class. In some cases your knowledge of personalities involved may suggest that children should write for less immediate or specific readers.
	Also, you may prefer to place less emphasis on choice of audience and to encourage imaginative writing for its own sake.
• Ask the children to write their story.	Encourage them to include a beginning, a middle and an end. Children who find it difficult to think of an original story can develop a story you have used to introduce the standard task.
• Remind them once to put in capital letters and full stops and make sure they understand the reminder, but do not show them where the capital letters and full stops should be placed.	You will need to decide the most appropriate point in the session at which to do this. Do not tell them where the capital letters and full stops should be placed.

At Key Stage 2, the 1994 Standard Task for Writing (AT3) was as follows:

Here are some starting points for short stories and a planning sheet to help you organise your ideas.

Your teacher will read out each one of the starting points, and tell you how to use the space for planning your story before you start to write it.

You will have 15 minutes in which to think about what to write and to jot down your ideas.

Your teacher will then give you another booklet to write in. You will have 45 minutes for writing your short story.

1. Changes

Near the beginning of the story, *Rachel on the Run*, Rachel looked in the mirror at her face. With a shock, she thought that 'it didn't feel recognisable or familiar at all'.

Imagine you wake up one morning to discover that you have completely changed and no-one recognises you.

Write a short story about what happens.

2. Time Travel

On a visit to a science museum you get into a time travel machine, even though it says 'Danger – Keep Out!'

You hope to re-visit some times in your own life, but the controls don't work properly and you get a few surprises.

Write a short story about your journey, being sure to tell your reader:
- **what you saw**
- **how you felt**
- **what happened to get you from one time to another.**

3. Story Starters

Choose **one** of these for your story.
EITHER:
Write a short story which opens with this sentence:
'Just go through that door and keep going until you reach the tunnel.'
OR:
Write a short story with the title:
The Long Road to Tomorrow.

Have you chosen **one** of the starting points? Now make a note of some of your ideas. Jot them down here, or turn over and use the Planning Sheet.

Planning sheet
*This is for **very brief notes** to help you plan your short story.*

Which title have you chosen to write about?

Setting

Characters (e.g. Who are they? What are they like?)

What makes the story **begin**?

What happens **next**?

How will your story **end**?

At Key Stage 3, pupils judged to be levels 1–3 in English are teacher-assessed only. In 1994 two test papers were used to assess levels 4–7, with an extension paper for levels 8–10. The first paper comprised an essay and comprehension; the second a Shakespeare paper. The following extract from the 1994 tests illustrates one of the questions from the Shakespeare paper in a prescribed scene from *Romeo and Juliet*:

ROMEO AND JULIET

Act 5 Scene 3, Lines 1–170

TASK

In this scene there are many moments of drama. Choose some of these and show how the tension and excitement build up to the tragic climax of Juliet's death.

To help you Before you begin to write, you should think about the following:
- where the scene is set;
- how the language of the characters shows their feelings;
- how the audience's feelings might change as they watch this scene;
- Juliet's last words and actions.

The assessment requirements of GCSE examinations at the end of Key Stage 4 has also attracted argument. John Major, when prime minister in the early 1990s, took a personal role in demanding that there should be formal examinations in all subjects. Prior to that many English teachers had chosen syllabus options that allowed for 100 per cent coursework. Again this is an area where a great deal of change has occurred and schools can provide information on the latest regulations. However, public examinations at Key Stage 4 are now the main means of assessing attainment in the National Curriculum.

There is one final point to make about English. All aspects of the subject are taught by all teachers. In a primary school this is recognized by teachers who will ensure that within, say, a science activity attention is given to progress in speaking and writing. At the secondary level, schools will have a policy for English and language across the curriculum and all teachers should be taking account of the development of skills and understanding that relates to the English curriculum. A paragraph on Use of Language forms part of the Common Requirements for all other National Curriculum subjects.

Mathematics

The content of the National Curriculum reflects much of the debate that has taken place over recent years about the introduction of 'modern mathematics' into the curriculum. The curriculum of the late 1960s and early 1970s was changed considerably with the introduction of sets, matrices, transformations, and vectors, and the removal of much of the traditional Euclidean geometry. At the same time, teaching for understanding rather than rote learning of skills was promoted. Over the last decade the process of investigating within mathematics and problem-solving has gained importance, and one attainment target in the latest version of the orders is devoted to the use and application of mathematics.

The curriculum has become streamlined, with more time devoted to ensuring that pupils' understanding of mathematics is enhanced in order that they may be more able to use and apply their skills to a variety of problems, both familiar and unfamiliar.

The National Curriculum is not designed to be a strait-jacket, but is the minimum that ought to be covered. If and when the situation dictates, pupils can be given the opportunity to study related areas outside the bounds of the National Curriculum. This is particularly necessary when teachers are working with high-attaining pupils.

The Programme of Study in mathematics is set out in key stages. The National Curriculum statutory orders make clear that all sections of the programme interrelate. They describe how developing mathematical language, selecting and using materials, and developing reasoning should be set in the context of the other areas of mathematics. Sorting, classifying, making comparisons, and searching for patterns should apply to work on number, shape and space, and handling data. The use of number should permeate work on measures and handling data.

The descriptions of what should be covered show a progression through the three stages. Under the heading number, for example, there is a section on developing an understanding of place value. Here are the entries for Key Stage 1, Key Stage 2, and the combined entry for Key Stages 3 and 4:

Key stage one

2. Developing an understanding of place value
a   count orally up to 10 and beyond, knowing the number names; count collections of objects, checking the total; count in steps of different sizes, *e.g. count on from 5 in steps of 2 or 3*; recognize sequences, including odd and even numbers;
b   read, write and order numbers, initially to 10, progressing up to 1000, developing an understanding that the position of a digit signifies its value; begin to approximate larger numbers to the nearest 10 or 100;
c   recognise and use in context simple fractions, including halves and quarters, decimal notation in recording money, and negative numbers, *e.g. a temperature scale, a number line, a calculator display*.

Key stage two

2. Developing an understanding of place value and extending the number system
a   read, write and order whole numbers, understanding that the position of a digit signifies its value; use their understanding of place value to develop methods of computation, to approximate numbers to the

nearest 10 or 100, and to multiply and divide by powers of 10 when there are whole-number answers;

b extend their understanding of the number system to negative numbers in context, and decimals with no more than two decimal places in the context of measurement and money;

c understand and use, in context, fractions and percentages to estimate, describe and compare proportions of a whole.

Key stages 3–4

2. Understanding place value and extending the number system
a understand and use the concept of place value in whole numbers and decimals, relating this to computation and the metric system of measurement;
b understand and use decimals, ratios, fractions and percentages, and the interrelationships between them; understand and use negative numbers;
c understand and use index notation, leading to standard form.

Attainment targets

There are four attainment targets in mathematics:

AT1.   Using and applying Mathematics
AT2.   Number and Algebra
AT3.   Shape, Space and Measures
AT4.   Handling data.

When you turn to AT2 Number, the part of the programme of study just described the level description that relates particularly to place value and extending the number system is:

Pupils count sets of objects reliably, and use mental recall of addition and subtraction facts to 10. They have begun to understand the place value of each digit in a number and use this to order numbers up to 100. They choose the appropriate operation when solving addition and subtraction problems They identify and use halves and quarters, such as half of a rectangle or a quarter of eight objects. They recognize sequences of numbers, including odd and even numbers.

Pupils who go beyond level 8 and perform at an exceptional level will:

understand and use rational and irrational numbers. They determine the bounds of intervals. Pupils understand and use direct and inverse proportion. In simplifying algebraic expressions, they use rules of indices for negative and fractional values. In finding formulae that approximately connect data, pupils express general laws in symbolic form. They solve problems using intersections and gradients of graphs.

Assessment

The assessment of the mathematics curriculum has been the subject of much controversy and debate. Testing of 7-year-olds at the end of Key Stage 1 took place for the first time in 1991 and at Key Stage 3 in 1992. The debate has raged over the nature of those tests, how much weight is given to teacher assessment, as well as the publication of 'league tables'. It has been argued that some aspects of mathematics cannot easily be assessed through traditional pencil-and-paper methods, and unless teacher assessment of these aspects is given greater credibility then only the nationally tested aspects of the curriculum will be taught.

As with English, these tests are likely to change from one year to the next and schools can provide further information. Examples of the sort of tests used at the end of each of key stages are set out below.

The Right Ingredients

Some children want to make Vegetable and Lentil Soup.

In the school garden they find	They need for the soup	How many will they have left **after** they have made the soup?
4 onions	1 onion	☐ onions
12 carrots	6 carrots	☐ carrots
20 potatoes	2 potatoes	☐ potatoes
6 leeks	4 leeks	☐ leeks
8 sticks of celery	2 sticks of celery	☐ sticks of celery

13. These charts show the colour of socks worn on one school day.

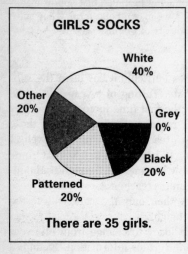

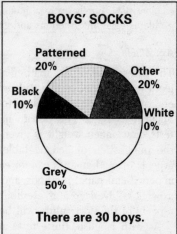

Ann says
"More girls than boys wore patterned socks."

Using both graphs give as many reasons as you can why she is right.

_____

_____

_____

40% of the 35 girls wore white socks.

Work out how many of the girls wore white socks. Show your working in the box below.

9. In a competition all boats have sails the same size.

(a) Work out the area
of the sail.
Show your working.

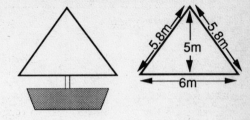

2 marks

The OZO company has designed these
three advertisements.

The competition has this rule:

Advertisements must cover **less** than 20% of the sail.

(b) The advertisement on this sail covers exactly 20%
of the sail.
Work out the area of the advertisement.
Show your working.

2 marks

(c) Work out the area of this advertisement to
see if it would be allowed on the sail.

Show your working.

2 marks

(d) Work out the area of this advertisement to see
if it would be allowed on the sail.

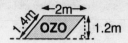

You will need to remember a formula to help
you answer this.
Use 3.14 or your calculator button for π.
Show your working.

3 marks

Science

Change in the science curriculum has also provoked controversy. All sorts of vested interests amongst teachers, parents, and the public at large can be threatened. Some research in the 1980s showed how the pupils themselves can prove resistant to innovation. In many ways this is a healthy reaction. The education system is susceptible to fads and fancies, and a degree of healthy scepticism is often warranted. From the 1960s onwards scientists, science teachers, and industrialists have argued strongly for science-curriculum reform. The Royal Society, for example, gave prestigious support to the reform proposals. In Chapter 2 the patchy, even non-existent provision in primary schools was commented on. At secondary level, the divisions into physics, chemistry, and biology meant that significant areas such as earth sciences or astronomy were often ignored. At the age of 14 some pupils dropped science completely, and others opted to continue the study of just one subject. Many boys chose physics and ignored biology. For girls it was the reverse. The National Curriculum for science attempts to put an end to these inconsistencies. School science may continue to be taught by specialists, especially at secondary level, but every pupil is now entitled to a balanced science curriculum, covering all the major scientific disciplines.

The programmes of study are set out in key stages. They describe both the processes of investigation and experimentation and the content. As with other subjects, the descriptions show progression from one key stage to another. For example, planning experiments at Key Stage 1 is set out as follows:

1. Planning experimental work
Pupils should be taught:
a   to turn ideas suggested to them, and their own ideas, into a form that can be investigated;
b   that thinking about what is expected to happen can be useful when planning what to do;
c   to recognise when a test or comparison is unfair.

Whereas at Key Stage 3 the requirements are more extensive and complex:

1.   Planning experimental procedures

Pupils should be taught:

a to use scientific knowledge and understanding to turn ideas suggested to them, and their own ideas, into a form that can be investigated;

b to carry out trial runs where appropriate;

c to make predictions where it is appropriate to do so;

d to consider, in simple context, key factors that need to be taken into account;

e to isolate the effect of changing one factor;

f to decide how many observations or measurements need to be made and what range they should cover;

g to consider contexts, *e.g. fieldwork*, where variables cannot readily be controlled, and to consider how evidence may be collected in these contexts;

h to select apparatus, equipment and techniques, taking account of safety requirements.

The same development can be seen when we compare the descriptions of what pupils at the different stages should be taught about humans as organisms:

Key stage 1

a to name the main external parts, *e.g. hand, elbow, knee*, of the human body;

b that humans need food and water to stay alive;

c that taking exercise and eating the right types and amount of food help humans to keep healthy;

d about the role of drugs as medicines;

e that humans can produce babies and these babies grow into children and then into adults;

f that humans have senses which enable them to be aware of the world around them.

Key stage 3

nutrition

a that balanced diets contain carbohydrates, proteins, fats, minerals, vitamins, fibre and water;

b some sources of the main food components in the diet;

c that food is used as a fuel during respiration to maintain the body's activity and as a raw material for growth and repair;

d the principles of digestion, including the role of enzymes;
e that the products of digestion are absorbed and waste material is egested;

circulation
f how blood acts as a transport medium and about the exchange of substances at the capillaries;

movement
g the role of the skeleton, joints and muscles in movement;
h the principle of antagonistic muscle pairs, *e.g. biceps and triceps*;

reproduction
i about the physical and emotional changes that take place during adolescence;
j the human reproductive system, including the menstrual cycle and fertilization;
k how the foetus develops in the uterus, including the role of the placenta;

breathing
l how lung structure enables gas exchange to take place;
m how smoking affects lung structure and gas exchange;

respiration
n that aerobic respiration involves the reaction in cells between oxygen and food used as a fuel;
o that during aerobic respiration glucose is broken down to carbon dioxide and water;
p to summarise aerobic respiration in a word equation;

Pupils should be taught:

health
q that the abuse of alcohol, solvents and other drugs affects health;
r that bacteria and viruses can affect health;
s that the body's natural defences may be enhanced by immunisation and medicines.

There are four attainment targets:

AT1.　Experimental and Investigative Science
AT2.　Life Processes and Living Things
AT3.　Materials and their Properties
AT4.　Physical Processes

The attainment targets are each developed from the four areas of the programme of study. For example, under AT1 Experimental and Investigative Science, level 2, at which a majority of Key Stage 1 pupils are likely to be working, it states:

Pupils respond to suggestions of how to find things out and, with help, make their own suggestions. They use simple equipment provided and make observations related to their task. They compare objects, living things and events they observe. They describe their observations and record them using simple tables where it is appropriate to do so. They say whether what happened was what they expected.

At level 6, the level which many Key Stage 3 pupils will reach:

Pupils use scientific knowledge and understanding to identify the key factors they need to consider and, where appropriate, to make predictions. They make observations and measure with precision a variety of quantities, using instruments with fine divisions. They make enough measurements and observations for the task. They choose scales for graphs that enable them to show appropriate data effectively. They identify measurements and observations that do not fit the main pattern or trend shown. They draw conclusions that are consistent with the evidence and explain these using scientific knowledge and undersanding.

The same progression is shown under AT2 Life Processes and Living Things:

Level 2

Pupils use their knowledge about living things to describe basic conditions, such as a supply of food, water, air or light, that animals and plants need in order to survive. They recognise that living things grow and reproduce. They sort living things into groups, using simple features. They describe the basis for their groupings in terms such as number of legs or shape of leaf. They recognise that different living things are found in different places, such as ponds or woods.

Level 6

Pupils use knowledge and understanding drawn from the key stage 3 programme of study, to describe and explain life processes and features of living things. They use appropriate scientific terminology when they describe life processes, such as respiration or photosynthesis, in animals and plants. They distinguish between related processes, such as pollination or fertilization. They describe simple cell structure and identify differences between cells, such as differences in structure between simple animal and plant cells. They describe some of the factors that cause variation between living things. They explain that the distribution and abundance of organisms in habitats are affected by environmental factors, such as the availability of light or water.

It is important to remember that investigations and experimenting happen throughout the science curriculum. An investigational activity in class, therefore, may well be developed through the sorts of activities required for understanding Life Processes and Living Things.

Science teaching has, then, changed significantly in recent years, and the National Curriculum reflects this. It is interesting to look at the advocacy for an approach to science that is broadly based, set out in the original recommendations for science in the National Curriculum.

The contribution of science in the school curriculum

Schools have an important role to play in helping children to understand the world they live in, and in preparing them for adult life and work. We are mindful of the value of our task in helping to equip these citizens of the next century with an education which should stand them in good stead in a world that will be very different from our own. We believe that science has an essential contribution to make in the following ways:

(1) Understanding scientific ideas

Scientists have developed a powerful body of knowledge about physical and biological phenomena. Science education should provide opportunities for all pupils to develop an understanding of key concepts and enable them to be used in unfamiliar situations. To allow this to happen, pupils need to understand and explore their use in a range of contexts; the study of pure or formal science by itself can lead to ineffective learning by many pupils. Technological applications, personal health or the environment can often provide contexts through which scientific concepts can be more effectively introduced and developed.

(2) *Developing scientific methods of investigation*

All pupils should be enabled to learn and to use scientific methods of investigation. They should have the opportunity to develop the skills of imaginative but disciplined enquiry which include systematic observation, making and testing hypotheses, designing and carrying out experiments competently and safely, drawing inferences from evidence, formulating and communicating conclusions in an appropriate form and applying them to new situations. Pupils should come to learn how to gain access to, and use selectively and appropriately, published scientific knowledge.

(3) *Relating science to other areas of knowledge*

Just as science cannot offer an adequate explanation of our world on its own, so science education needs to relate to other areas of the school curriculum. Pupils should be encouraged to recognise and value the contribution which science can make to other areas of learning, and the knowledge, skills and inspiration which scientists can derive from other activities.

(4) *Understanding the contribution science makes to society*

Pupils should be encouraged to study the practical applications of science and technology and the ways they are changing the nature of our society and our economy. They should be helped to explore some of the moral dilemmas that scientific discoveries and technological developments can cause. Science education should encourage all pupils to appreciate their responsibilities as members of society and give them the confidence to make a positive contribution to it.

(5) *Recognising the contribution science education makes to personal development*

Productive learning needs the right conditions. Successful science and technology education requires pupils to combine interest and curiosity with a responsible attitude towards safety, and a respect for living organisms and the physical environment. It should help to develop other attitudes such as a willingness to accept uncertainty, to co-operate with others, to give honest reports, and to think critically. A study of science is an important dimension of health education, and pupils should become aware of its relevance to matters of personal and public health. Understanding and clarifying one's own thinking is often an essential part of learning. Throughout their science education, pupils should be encouraged to develop their powers of reasoning by reflecting on their own understanding, and by appreciating that learning may involve a change in the way they think about, explain and do things.

(6) Appreciating the nature of scientific knowledge

Pupils should further their understanding of science by exploring the social and historical contexts of scientific discoveries. Through this they can begin to appreciate the powerful but provisional nature of scientific explanation, and the process by which models are created, tested and modified in the light of evidence. Most important of all, they will be reminded of the excitement of discovery that has been the continual inspiration of all scientists.

Recent developments in our understanding of the way children learn have been incorporated into the programmes and advice for the teaching of science. For example, practical investigative approaches are given a prominent place through the first attainment target. Investigative abilities are seen to develop as the children mature and as they are brought into contact with new contexts and areas of knowledge. Skills of investigation and knowledge of the attainment targets are seen to develop alongside positive attitudes towards the subject. A lively and imaginative science programme can help children develop the following:

- curiosity
- respect for evidence
- willingness to tolerate uncertainty
- critical reflection
- perseverance
- creativity and inventiveness
- open-mindedness
- sensitivity to the living and non-living environment
- co-operation with others.

A parent who went to school in the 1950s, 1960s, or even 1970s would probably find that science is the subject in which there has been the most significant change. Experiments and investigations should now feature in most lessons. The situation where the teacher demonstrates an experiment which the pupils then try to copy exactly will be very rare. Experimentation is much more open-ended than it used to be.

Assessment

Assessment in science has been less controversial than in English, but problems have occurred. How, for example, to produce a fair test. This occurs in all subjects, but science is a subject where a considerable amount of research has taken place. An example of one finding that makes test-setting difficult is in the tricky area of boy–girl differences. A few years ago it was found that the context of a test could advantage either boys or girls. Even if the test was ostensibly about a gender-neutral skill such as 'observing' the context in which the test was carried out is significant. For example, if an investigation is based on foodstuffs, girls might do better, whereas with electrical circuits boys could be advantaged. This is a complex area affecting all parts of the curriculum and it could lead to significant changes in the way tests are set up and assessed. Schools can give up-to-date information on this. Examples of tests at the end of Key Stages 2–3 are set out below.

A final assessment issue relates to GCSE. The National Curriculum recommends strongly that the vast majority of pupils take either a double science GCSE, now by far the most popular option, or biology, chemistry, and physics, the traditional option but now less popular, as it can take up too much curriculum time and restrict the choice of other subjects, for example Latin or economics, that are outside the National Curriculum. The National Curriculum orders in science are structured to allow pupils to take a single science programme. But this is not encouraged, and double science looks like being the favoured option for some time to come.

These questions are taken from recent Key Stage 2 and Key Stage 3 tests in science. The first two questions are for Key Stage 2 pupils.

17. Here are two fish.
The parts of the fish have labels.

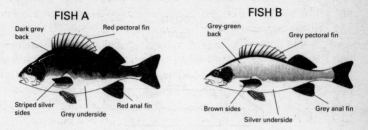

FISH A

Dark grey back   Red pectoral fin

Striped silver sides   Grey underside   Red anal fin

FISH B

Grey-green back   Grey pectoral fin

Brown sides   Silver underside   Grey anal fin

Use the key below to find out what the name of each fish is.

Has the fish got red anal fins?

Yes — Is the fish striped?

    Yes — It is a perch

    No — It is a roach

No — Is the underside silver?

    Yes — Is the back grey-green?

        Yes — It is a minnow

        No — It is a shark

    No — It is a tench

a. Fish A is a _____

b. Fish B is a _____

Circuit

25. Here is a picture of a switch.

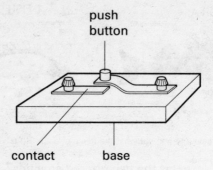

You have to make the **base**, the **contact** and the **push-button** for the switch.
You can use these materials.

wood   plastic   brass   steel

 Complete these sentences with the name of <u>**ONE**</u> material you could use.

a. I would make the **base** using _____

b. I would make the **contact** using _____

c. I would make the **push-button** using _____

11. The drawings show five types of plant and animal cell.

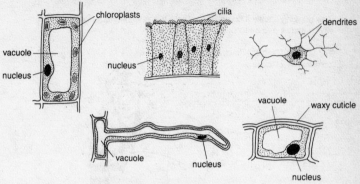

Each cell has a special feature or structure.

Draw a line to join each feature or structure to its function.

One has been done for you.

4 marks

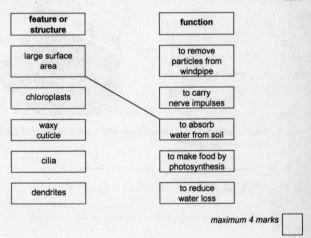

feature or structure	function
large surface area	to remove particles from windpipe
chloroplasts	to carry nerve impulses
waxy cuticle	to absorb water from soil
cilia	to make food by photosynthesis
dendrites	to reduce water loss

maximum 4 marks

18. Garden waste can decay to form compost.

The drawing shows a compost tumbler. It is attached to a metal frame which allows it to be turned over.

Turning the tumbler allows air to reach all the waste. It will make good compost in 21 days.

(a) Name **two** types of living organism which help the decay of the waste in a compost tumbler.

1 mark

1. _____

1 mark

2. _____

(b) Give **two** conditions which are needed for waste to decay.

1 mark

1. _____

1 mark

2. _____

maximum 4 marks

6 The Foundation Subjects: Design and Technology, History, Geography, Modern Foreign Languages, Art, Music, Physical Education, and Information Technology

This group of subjects represents the remaining foundation subjects of the National Curriculum. A modern foreign language does not have to be taught in Key Stages 1 and 2.

Four of the subjects: design and technology, history, geography, and a modern foreign language, are set out like English, mathematics, and science, with programmes of study and attainment targets divided into eight levels. The remaining four subjects: art, music, physical education, and information technology have end-of-key-stage descriptions for the Attainment Targets as compared to the more detailed eight levels.

Design and technology

The introduction of design and technology into the primary and secondary curriculum is one of the major innovations of the National Curriculum. For some time a growing body of opinion had been arguing for technology to be given far greater importance at all levels of schooling. This was acknowledged in the first consultation document on the National Curriculum, and the technology working party was the first to be set up after the core foundation subject groups. The final report it produced was one of the least controversial, perhaps in part because so few people had had direct experience of the subject in their own school-days. The foreword of the document that made the final recommendations to the secretary of state underlined why every child should study technology:

Technology is the one subject in the national curriculum that is directly concerned with generating ideas, making and doing. In emphasizing the importance of practical capability, and providing opportunities for pupils to develop their powers to innovate, to make decisions, to create new solutions, it can play a unique role. Central to this role is the task of providing balance in a curriculum based on academic subjects—a balance in which the creative and practical capabilities of pupils can be fully developed and inter-related. The subject has a crucial part to play in helping pupils to develop these important personal qualities and competences.

Whilst the contribution of technology to the personal development of individuals is very important, of equal importance is its role in helping pupils to respond to the employment needs of business and industry. Pupils will become aware of technological development, and the way in which technology is changing the workplace and influencing lifestyles. They will learn that technological change cannot be reversed, and will understand its enormous power. Knowledge of technology enables citizens to be prepared to meet the needs of the 21st century and to cope with a rapidly changing society.

Although the first report was uncontroversial, and whilst almost everyone appeared to recognize the importance of design and technology, the first few years of a National Curriculum in the subject area were highly controversial. You will note that the quote above only refers to technology, the subject title in the first statutory order which embraced the two areas of 'Information Technology' and 'Design and Technology'. Information Technology has a contribution to make to all subjects, and this curriculum area has now been amended to the dual 'Design and Technology'. A large body of opinion was critical of the early plans for the subject, because of its lack of a significant practical 'making' element. In trying to establish the academic basis for the subject the applied nature of the knowledge base had, it was suggested, been downgraded. There were also difficulties in schools. At a primary level few teachers had experience of the subject. At secondary level the teaching of technology was entrusted to a very disparate group of practical subject areas with very different traditions. Craft, design, and technology (CDT) teachers had traditionally little contact with home economics or business studies specialists. Subjects such as science and mathematics have a well-developed status in the curriculum. For new subjects such as design and technology that status will take some time to establish.

The programme of study refers to designing and making skills as well as the knowledge and understanding that underpins such skills. At Key Stage 1 the curriculum in designing skills must ensure that pupils:

a draw on their own experience to help generate ideas;
b clarify their ideas through discussion;
c develop their ideas through shaping, assembling and rearranging materials and components;
d develop and communicate their design ideas by making freehand drawings, and by modelling their ideas in other ways, *e.g. by using actual materials and components with temporary fixings*;
e make suggestions about how to proceed;
f consider their design ideas as these develop, and identify strengths and weaknesses.

At Key Stage 3 the list lengthens and becomes more complex:

Pupils should be taught to:
a identify appropriate sources of information that will help with their designing;
b use design briefs to guide design thinking;
c develop a specification for their product;
d consider the needs and values of intended users and develop criteria for their design to guide thinking and form a basis for evaluation;
e generate design proposals that match stated design criteria and modify proposals to improve them;
f consider the aesthetics, function, safety, reliability and cost of their designs;
g take account of the working characteristics and properties of materials and components when deciding how and when to use them;
h prioritise and reconcile decisions on materials and components, production, time and costs within design proposals;
i take account of the restrictions imposed by the capacities and limitations of tools and equipment;
j explore, develop and communicate their design ideas by modelling their ideas in an increasing variety of ways, including the use of IT [information technology];
k develop a clear idea of what has to be done and propose an outline

plan, which includes alternative methods of proceeding if things go wrong;

l evaluate their design ideas as these develop, bearing in mind the users and the purposes for which the product is intended, and indicate ways of improving their ideas.

Under Knowledge and Understanding the Programme of Study describes what should be taught about materials and components, systems and control, structures, products and applications, quality, and health and safety. Taking the example of structures, at Key Stage 1 pupils should know how to make structures they have made more stable and able to withstand greater loads. At Key Stage 3 there are five categories of requirements. Pupils must be taught:

a to recognise and use structures in their products;
b that excessive loads can cause structures to fail by bending, buckling and twisting;
c to use simple tests to determine the effects of excessive loads;
d to devise suitable methods to reinforce their structures and relate these and other techniques to familiar structures;
e to understand that forces, such as compression and tension, produce different effects, and to take account of these in making their products.

There are two attainment targets:

AT1. Designing
AT2. Making

The level 2 description of what could be achieved says that when designing:

pupils use their experiences of using materials, techniques and products to help generate ideas. They use models and pictures to develop and communicate their designs. They reflect on their ideas and suggest improvements.

and when making:

pupils select from a range of materials, tools and techniques, explaining their choices. They manipulate tools safely and assemble and join materials in a variety of ways. They make judgements about the outcomes of their work.

The higher level 6, however, says that when designing:

pupils generate ideas that draw on a wider range of sources of information, including those not immediately related to the task, and an understanding of the form and function of familiar products. They develop criteria for their designs, which take into account appearance, function, safety, reliability and the users and purposes for which they are intended, and use these to formulate a design proposal. They make preliminary models to explore and test their design thinking, and use formal drawing methods to communicate their intentions.

and when making:

pupils produce plans that outline the implications of their design decisions, and suggest alternative methods of proceeding if first attempts should fail. They are becoming increasingly skilful in the use of the techniques and processes identified in the key stage 3 Programme of Study, and use tools and equipment to work materials precisely. They evaluate their products in use and identify ways of improving them.

In fact, all the attainment targets begin the level description with the phrase *when designing and making* because in practice the two processes are so closely interrelated.

The prime rationale for design and technology is the process approach, because it can extend over so many different subjects and contexts. Established subjects such as craft, design, and technology (CDT), business studies, home economics, and computer studies are all incorporated into this approach to technology. Other subjects, aspects of art, mathematics, and science for example, could also be included.

In designing and making different products can be included:

- artefacts (objects made by people);
- systems (sets of objects or activities which together perform a task); and
- environments (surroundings made, or developed, by people).

These are not mutually exclusive. For example, a puppet could be regarded as an artefact with a particular finish and appearance, or as a system if the emphasis is on the mechanism for articulation. A greenhouse could be considered as an artefact (in relation to a shed), a system (in relation to temperature stability), or an environment for plants. What is intended is that pupils should consider a range of products. They should also consider the design of existing products and applications which might inform their own ideas.

Similarly, they should work with a range of materials. At Key Stage 1 this would include reclaimed material, textiles, food, and construction kits. At Key Stage 3 pupils design and make products focusing on different contexts and materials, such as 'resistant materials' (wood, metal, and plastics) and 'compliant materials' (textiles and plastic sheet) and/or food. The use of food and textiles, therefore, is not compulsory at Key Stage 3, although there should be one alternative to resistant materials. Taken together, works on the different materials should include work with control systems and structures.

Some of the titles and phrases have a ring of unfamiliarity about them. 'Consider appearance, function and reliability' or 'consider the needs and values of intended users', for example, have only just come into the terminology of professional educationists, let alone the lay public.

Technology: Northern Ireland

The technology curriculum in Northern Ireland is known as 'Technology and Design' and is significantly different from that of England and Wales. Information Technology is a designated cross-curricular theme in the province and so is not linked to technology. There is only one attainment target, Technology and Design Capability, as there is a strong emphasis on the need to consider technological activity as a whole rather than as separate and discrete parts. The attainment targets state that:

Pupils should develop the ability to design products. In particular, they should develop, in parallel, their ability:

- to apply knowledge and understanding;
- to communicate effectively;
- to manipulate a range of materials and components to make products;
- to use energy to drive and control products they design.

The knowledge and understanding which is required in Technology and Design is drawn primarily from Science. Communication of designing emphasizes the use of computers and the strand associated with control emphasizes both electronics and pneumatics as well as computer control. The 'range of materials' includes metal, plastics, textiles, and wood. Food is not a 'material' in the Northern Ireland technology curriculum, although Home Economics does have a separate place at Key Stages 3 and 4. The importance of social, economic, and environmental factors is stressed in every key stage and there is a strong emphasis on the importance of Technology and Design to wealth creation.

History

National Curriculum history has precipitated a great deal of public controversy over *what* history should be taught in schools. This was a subject which produced more controversy and print in the pages of the newspapers and journals than any other, with the possible exception of English. At stake was the place of 'British' history in the school curriculum, together with the place of facts—names, dates, people, and events—in teaching history. On the former, it is interesting to consider the different programmes of study for England, Northern Ireland, and Wales, which are summarized below.

Also at the heart of the controversy was the debate around history as 'content' versus 'skills'. The 1970s saw the development of a new rationale for teaching history as teachers and pupils reacted against syllabuses which were chronological outline surveys of British political history. This 'new' history emphasized historical methodology and a syllabus which was 'relevant' to the lives of young people. Modern world history and local history were introduced, together with an emphasis on enquiry-based learning.

Critics of the 'new' history saw the subject being reduced to an endless stream of source evaluation and empathy exercises which paid no attention to historical facts. Critics of 'facts' in history argued that concentration on this would reduce history to a game of mastermind. This dichotomy between historical skills and facts is, in fact, a false one. Facts, that is, names, dates, events, and so on, provide information about the past which is an essential part of history, but they do not in themselves constitute history or provide an understanding of the past. Any study of history needs to include both, that is, a thorough knowledge of past events, together with an understanding of historical method (the way in which historians carry out their work). History also crucially involves a range of explanations and understandings.

The requirements of the statutory orders

The statutory orders for history apply to Key Stages 1, 2, and 3. History is optional at Key Stage 4 and pupils follow a variety of GCSF syllabuses which all meet the national criterion for history.

The format of the National Curriculum history is similar to the orders for the other subjects in that it lays down the programmes of study and the attainment targets. The Programme of Study in history is set out under the headings Areas of Study for Key Stage 1 and Areas of Study for Key Stages 2 and 3, and Key Elements. The former represents the 'content' that must be covered, and the latter the knowledge and understanding about processes and skills. At Key Stages 2 and 3 the Programmes of Study also specify that pupils should be given the opportunity to study aspects of the past through different dimensions. For example, in outline and in depth at Key Stage 2 and in outline, in depth, and through a local context at Key Stage 3. At both key stages pupils have to be given opportunities to study aspects of the histories of England, Ireland, Scotland, and Wales; and where appropriate, the history of Britain should be set in its European and World context. Pupils also have to be given opportunities to study history from a variety of perspectives—political; economic, technological, and scientific; social; religious; cultural and aesthetic.

There are five Key Elements which have to be covered across each key stage. These build progression into pupils' development of historical understanding and cover chronology, range and depth of historical knowledge and understanding, interpretations of history, historical enquiry, and the organization and communication of history. This structure represents a balance between the competing schools of thought described above. The English and Welsh National Curriculum in this subject is published separately. In England, at Key Stage 1:

pupils should be taught about past events of different types, including events from the history of Britain, *e.g. notable local and national events, events in other countries, events that have been remembered and commemorated by succeeding generations, such as centenaries, religious festivals, anniversaries, the Gunpowder Plot, the Olympic Games.*

This comes under the Area of Study description. Alongside that, under the Key Elements, skills of historical enquiry are listed as being:

a   how to find out about aspects of the past from a range of sources of information, including artefacts, pictures and photographs, adults talking about their own past, written sources, and buildings and sites;

b   to ask and answer questions about the past.

At Key Stage 3 examples of study units within the programmes of study include:

Britain 1750–circa 1900	An overview of some of the main events, personalities developments in the period and, in particular, how worldwide expansion, industrialisation and political developments combined to shape modern Britain. Pupils should be taught about an aspect of the period in depth.
The twentieth-century world	An overview of some of the main events, personalities and developments of the twentieth century and how they, and total war in particular, have shaped the modern world. Pupils should be taught about an aspect of the period in depth.

And at that age, pupils should be able, in terms of historical enquiry for example, to:

a   investigate independently aspects of the periods studied, using a range of sources of information, including documents and printed sources, artefacts, pictures, photographs and films, music and oral accounts, buildings and sites;

b   to ask and answer significant questions, to evaluate sources in their historical context, identify sources for an investigation, collect and record information relevant to a topic and reach conclusions.

In Key Stages 2 and 3 all pupils must follow a series of study units. These cover:

Key stage 2

Romans, Anglo-Saxons
and Vikings in Britain
Life in Tudor times
either Victorian Britain
or Britain since 1930
Ancient Greece
Local history

A past non-European society chosen from the following list:
- Ancient Egypt;
- Mesopotamia, *e.g. Ancient Sumer or the Assyrian Empire*;
- the Indus Valley;
- the Maya;
- Benin;
- the Aztecs.

Key stage 3

Medieval realms:
Britain 1066–1500
The making of the
United Kingdom:
crowns, parliaments and
peoples 1500–1750
Britain 1750–circa 1900
The twentieth-century *Examples could include: Islamic civilizations*
world *(seventh to sixteenth centuries); Imperial China from the First Emperor to Kublai Khan; India from the Mogul Empire to the coming of the British; the civilisations of Peru; indigenous peoples of North America; black peoples of the Americas; Japan under the Shoguns.* The society taught must be different to that selected in Key Stage 2.

Wales

In Wales, the five Key Elements to be developed through the study of history are very similar to those in the English Orders: chronological awareness, range and depth of historical knowledge and understanding, interpretations of history, historical enquiry, and organization and communication. Pupils also have to be given, across the Key Stages 2 and 3, the opportunities to study history from a variety of aspects and perspectives. For example:

pupils should be given opportunities to study aspects of the past in depth, aspects of Welsh and British history, set, where appropriate, in their European and world contexts. In their study of British history, pupils should be given opportunities, where appropriate to consider the historical experiences of the countries which make up the British Isles; history from a variety of perspectives: political, economic, social and cultural.

At Key Stage 1 pupils should be taught about everyday life in the past, lives of famous people, and past events—local, such as St David's Day and national, such as the Olympic Games.

Alongside the areas of study, under the Key Elements, the skills of historical enquiry are listed as being:

a   to be taught about the ways in which they can find out about the past from a range of historical sources, including artefacts, buildings and sites, adults talking about their own past, visual sources, *e.g. pictures, paintings, photographs and films, songs, books and other written sources*;

b   to ask and answer questions about the past, *e.g. interview grandparents and other adults, choose questions to ask about sources*.

At Key Stage 3 examples of study units within the programmes of study include:

Wales in Industrial Britain c.1760–1914   Pupils should be taught about the social, economic and technological transformation of Wales and Britain during a period of industrialisation. They should be taught about the process of industrialisation, its effects, and the social and political responses to them in Wales and Britain.

The Twentieth Century World   Pupils should be taught about aspects of twentieth century world history. They should be taught about major events and developments which have shaped the modern world, through studies of the impact of world war and changes in twentieth century society, including the role of significant individuals;

and at that age, pupils should be able, in terms of historical enquiry for example, to:

a   investigate historical topics independently and to use and evaluate a range of historical sources in their historical contexts, including documents, artefacts, visual sources, buildings and sites, music and oral accounts;

b   to ask and answer significant questions, select sources from historical enquiry, collect and record information and reach reasoned conclusions, *e.g. identify hypotheses after an initial study of sources, suggest what and where information relevant to a particular enquiry might be found, refine questions in the light of an initial enquiry, initiate and structure investigations with greater independence.*

The series of study units which all pupils must follow at Key Stages 2 and 3 cover:

Key Stage 2

Life in Early Wales and Britain
Life in Wales and Britain in Tudor and Stuart Times
Life in Modern Wales and Britain
A Study of a Historical Issue or Topic in a Local Context
A Study of a Historical Theme   chosen from the following list:
- Houses and households
- Ships and sailors
- Writing and reading
- Food and farming
- Land and air transport
- Castles or religious buildings
- Life and beliefs in the ancient world.

Key Stage 3

Wales and Britain in the Medieval World *c.*100–1500
Wales and Britain in the Early Modern World—*c.*1500–1760
Wales in Industrial Britain *c.*1760–*c.*1914
The Twentieth Century World
Pupils should then be taught TWO Extension units:
A Study of a Historical Issue or Topic in a Local Context
A Study of a Historical Theme (in depth)
chosen from: • Exploration and encounters
- War and society
- The world of work
- Revolutions
- Frontiers
- Migration and emigration
- Empires
- Sport and society.

There is only one Attainment Target in history in England and Wales. This is divided into level descriptions which describe the types and range of attainment that pupils working at different levels should characteristically demonstrate. They are used for summative purposes only, say at the end of the key stage or at the end of a year. For example, at level 4:

Pupils demonstrate factual knowledge and understanding of aspects of the history of Britain and other countries, drawn from the Key Stage 2 or Key Stage 3 programme of study. They use this to describe the characteristic features of past societies and periods, and to identify changes within and across periods. They describe some of the main events, people and changes. They give some reasons for, and results of, the main events and changes. They show how some aspects of the past have been represented and interpreted in different ways. They are beginning to select and combine information from sources. They are beginning to produce structured work, making appropriate use of dates and terms.

Northern Ireland
Key Stage 1

At Key Stage 1, as in England and Wales, the programme of study consists of one history study unit. This introduces pupils to the idea of the past through stories, artefacts, visual material, and the study of their personal histories and home life, and the study of changes in the recent past in relation to their parents, grandparents, and their own locality.

At Key Stages 2 and 3 there are two types of History Study Units (HSUs): the core study units covering selected areas of Irish, British, European, and world history which must be taught in chronological sequence, and the school-designed history study units (SDUs). The planning of these is left to the school in order to allow teachers to draw on their own particular knowledge and enthusiasms, but they have to meet specified ground rules to ensure compatibility with the HSUs.

Key Stage 2

There are six history study units, comprising three compulsory core history study units and three school-designed units. The core study units are:

- Life in Early Times;
- The Vikings;
- Life in Victorian Times.

The school-designed units are:

- a Study in Development—for example, Transport through the ages;
- a Study in Depth—for example, Aspects of the Roman World;
- a Local Study—for example, a local canal.

Key Stage 3

There are seven history study units comprising three compulsory core history study units and four school-designed units. The core study units are:

- (Y8) The Norman impact on the medieval world;
- (Y9) Britain, Ireland, and Europe from the late sixteenth to the early eighteenth centuries;
- (Y10) Ireland and British Politics in the late nineteenth and the early twentieth centuries.

The school-designed units are:

- a study in depth, for example, The American Frontier;
- a line of development study, for example, Energy;
- a local study, for example, an archaeological site study, such as Nendrum (linked to an introduction to history and its sources);
- a study related to the twentieth century, for example, The Russian Revolution.

(Examples taken from Northern Ireland Curriculum Council—Guidance Materials History, 1991).

Key Stage 4

At Key Stage 4 there are two core history study units:

- Core 1: Northern Ireland and its Neighbours since 1920;
- Core 2: Conflict and Co-operation in Europe since 1919.

Geography

Geography, like other subjects in the National Curriculum, can be the subject of lively national debate. Some of the critics of contemporary education, here and abroad, have pointed to children's inadequate knowledge of countries and cities as evidence of declining standards. At the same time, others have pointed to the futility of what has been termed a 'capes and bays' approach to the subject. The ability to reel off a list of capital cities or major rivers, it is argued, is as empty an exercise as giving the dates of kings and queens. Inevitably the National Curriculum in geography attracted some of this debate, although in a more muted form than in subjects such as English or history.

The context of and approach to teaching geography have undergone significant changes in the last few decades. Many parents will remember drawing detailed regional maps, with symbols to show where coal mines or shoe manufacturing existed. They might also remember diagrams of V-shaped valleys gouged out by the ice of a glacial period. An interest in regions and the physical characteristics of the earth still exists, but in the context of some new perspectives that have profoundly influenced the way the subject is approached. There have been, for example, important developments to strengthen the scientific, and particularly mathematical, basis of the subject. Secondly, in a contrasting but complementary way, there has been a move to focus on issues and problems that go beyond the particular characteristics of regions or countries. The decline in world stocks of national fuel resources, poverty across significant parts of the globe, and the economic interdependence between developed and underdeveloped countries would be three examples.

A contemporary definition of the subject was made by the working group which prepared the National Curriculum geography report.

1. Geography explores the relationship between the Earth and its peoples through the study of *place*, *space*, and *environment*. Geographers ask the questions *where* and *what*; also *how* and *why*.
2. The study of *place* seeks to describe and understand not only the location of the physical and human features of the Earth, but also the processes, systems, and interrelationships that create or influence those features.
3. The study of *space* seeks to explore the relationships between places and patterns of activity arising from the use people make of the physical settings where they live and work.
4. The study of the *environment* embraces both its physical and human dimensions. Thus it addresses the resources, sometimes scarce and fragile, that the Earth provides, and on which all life depends; the

impact on those resources of human activities; and the wider social, economic, political, and cultural consequences of the interrelationship between the two.

In geography both content and skills required are set out. In the Programme of Study these are listed under the headings: Places, Thematic Studies, and Geographical Skills. At Key Stage 1, for example, pupils must look at how the quality of the environment can be sustained. This could include study of how urban areas could be pedestrianized, or the advantages of cycle lanes. They must also study the locality of the school and a contrasting locality in the United Kingdom or abroad. But in doing this they must practice geographical skills such as local fieldwork activities, drawing perhaps a map of the school and immediate vicinity, or a plan of the town centre.

At Key Stage 3 these same skills are more developed. For example, in investigating places and themes pupils should be given the opportunity to:

a identify geographical questions and issues and establish an appropriate sequence of investigation;
b identify the evidence required and collect, record and present it;
c analyse and evaluate the evidence, draw conclusions and communicate findings.

At Key Stage 3 all pupils must study two countries other than the United Kingdom. One country must be chosen from each of two lists:

List A	List B
Australia and New Zealand	Africa
Europe	Asia (excluding Japan)
Japan	South and Central America
North America	(including the Carbbean)
Russian Federation	

At Key Stage 3 there are also eight themes prescribed:

Tectonic processes
Geomorphological processes
Weather and climate
Ecosystems

Population
Settlement
Economic activities
Development

As with history, there is only one attainment target, titled Geography.

Modern Foreign Languages in the National Curriculum

For the first time in its history, MFL is shedding its élitist image. Pupils of all levels of attainment between the ages of 11 and 16 are enjoying a wider-reaching and more varied diet of activities than ever before. Foreign languages are at last, in our multilingual society, being given the status they deserve. One major factor in this recognition is their inclusion as a foundation subject in the National Curriculum. In effect, this requires all pupils aged between 11 and 16 to study a foreign language. In Wales, the requirement only applies to pupils in Key Stage 3, and at Key Stage 4 in England pupils may follow a short course of study to fulfil the requirement.

Traditionally, the language most frequently offered by schools as a first foreign language has been French. Recently government resources have been invested in changing this state of affairs in favour of a much more diverse pattern, and now it is not unusual to find schools which have 'diversified', offering German, Italian, or Spanish as a first foreign language. Yet concerns about staffing these hitherto lesser-taught languages are far from resolved, since the majority of linguists entering the teaching profession are till French graduates. The issue of pupils changing schools, with a resultant change of foreign language, is also potentially problematic.

Schools are required by the National Curriculum order to offer their pupils a European Community language and may, in addition, offer a non-European Community language. Nineteen languages from which schools may choose are listed (those asterisked are official European Community languages): Arabic, Bengali, Chinese (Cantonese or Mandarin), Danish*, French*, Greek (modern)*, Gujarati, Hebrew (modern), Hindi, Italian*, Japanese, Punjabi, Portuguese*, Russian, Spanish*, Turkish, Urdu.

The teaching of languages like many other subjects has changed significantly in recent years. Much more attention is being given to *communicating* rather than just having a written, grammatical, or silent reading understanding. The structure of employment in the next century is likely to have a much more European and international character. Already the number of pupils following languages courses post-16 is increasing and the ability to communicate in a second and third language could become crucial to many jobs. The National Curriculum programmes of study reflect this emphasis on communication and require teachers to use the target language as much as possible in all teaching activities. The curriculum is set out in two parts which cover the skills and broad topic areas to be developed at Key Stages 3 and 4 (remember, modern foreign languages are not, at present, part of the National Curriculum at Key Stages 1 and 2):

Part 1:   Learning and Using the Target Language;
Part 2:   Areas of Experience ('Contexts for Learning' in Northern Ireland).

The two parts are designed to be taught together so that there is an interrelation of skills and content.

Part 1 is subdivided into five sections—communicating in the target language; language skills; language learning skills; knowledge of language, and cultural awareness. Under each heading, language learning opportunities which pupils should be given are listed. For instance, under 'communicating in the target language', pupils should be given the opportunity to:

a   communicate with each other in pairs and groups, and with their teacher;
b   use language for real purposes, as well as to practise skills;
c   develop their understanding and skills through a range of language activities, *e.g. games, role-play, surveys and other investigations*;
d   take part in imaginative and creative activities, *e.g. improvised drama*;
e   use everyday classroom events as a context for spontaneous speech;
f   discuss their own ideas, interests and experiences and compare them with those of others;
g   listen, read or view for personal interest and enjoyment, as well as for information;
h   listen and respond to different types of spoken language;
i   read handwritten and printed texts of different types and of varying lengths and, where appropriate, read aloud;
j   produce a variety of types of writing;

k use a range of resources for communicating, *e.g. telephone, electronic mail, fax, letters*.

And five areas of experience in which the language could be used are set out in Part 2:

A. Everyday activities
B. Personal and social life
C. The world around us
D. The world of work
E. The international world.

There are four attainment targets:

AT1. Listening and Responding
AT2. Speaking
AT3. Reading and Responding
AT4. Writing.

The four targets allow each of the level descriptions to be succinct and precise. In AT2 Speaking, for example, at level 1:

Pupils respond briefly, with single words or short phrases, to what they see and hear. Their pronunciation may be approximate, and they may need considerable support from a spoken model and from visual cues

whereas beyond level 8 the 'Exceptional performance' description requires pupils to be able to:

discuss a wide range of factual and imaginative topics, giving and seeking personal views and opinions in informal and formal situations. They speak fluently, with consistently accurate pronunciation, and show an ability to vary intonation. They give clear messages and make few errors.

Because of the very different structure of some languages these common requirements have, in certain circumstances, to be adapted. Within the National Curriculum orders qualifications are made for pupils studying Chinese (Mandarin or Cantonese) and Japanese.

In the Northern Ireland orders Part 1 of the programmes of study is divided into 'general skills', and 'language-specific skills'. The language-specific skills are similar to those outlined in the English and Welsh orders but the general skills include:

- personal and social skills;
- transferable learning skills;
- vocational skills.

These are not separated in the English and Welsh orders but are largely subsumed under the heading 'Learning and Using the Target Language'.

Art

Art, along with music and physical education, was in the final group of subjects to be set out in statutory orders laid before parliament. The National Curriculum has two attainment targets in England:

AT1.   Investigating and Making;
AT2.   Knowledge and Understanding;

whereas in Welsh schools the secretary of state for Wales decided to adopt three attainment targets: Understanding, Making, and Investigating.

The working party that prepared the recommendations for art within the National Curriculum recognized that, in primary schools, art is usually taught by general class teaching. In cases of best practice, they suggest, the head and teachers share aims and objectives, often expressed in a clearly stated policy document. The continuity provided by individual teachers planning within that agreed policy is an important factor. In the most successful schools, the place of art education in the curriculum is understood and appropriate teaching and organization provided. In particular, the staff:

- stimulate pupils' imagination and inventiveness; for example, making classrooms visually stimulating, and providing enrichment from displays, books, works and visits by artists, craft-workers and designers;
- give clear guidance, where appropriate, having analysed the steps that pupils need to take to gain in skill or understand a concept;
- provide opportunities for pupils to develop proficiency in a limited range of hand tools and materials, both traditional and new, while avoiding the superficiality which can come from working with too diverse an array of art materials and techniques;
- ensure that pupils produce work in both two and three dimensions—the latter being particularly important for tactile learning, understanding of scale and proportion and the handling of tools;
- balance the activity of making art, craft and design with opportunities for pupils to reflect upon and discuss their own work and the work of others;

- develop pupils' drawing abilities to the point where they are at ease using drawing as a tool; for example, to aid thinking;
- develop pupils' confidence, value of and pleasure in art, craft and design;
- appreciate and value pupils' individual responses in their own right, rather than seeing them as a form of inferior adult art.

At the secondary level the report was more critical, and HMI reports were quoted that showed strong contrasts from school to school in what students achieved, and the range of activities provided. Standards in painting, for example, were not as high as in drawing, and in over half the schools surveyed three-dimensional work was restricted to ceramics. Most schools, the report suggested, give inadequate attention to the appreciation and critical judgement of work by artists, craftworkers, and designers. The National Curriculum report goes on to suggest:

The national curriculum provides an opportunity to bring about important advances in the teaching of art, craft and design in schools. In many primary and some secondary schools there have been traditional preoccupations which have inhibited the development of a rich and rewarding art curriculum. In these schools, a narrow range of activities has been dominant, centred almost entirely on 'making' and accompanied by an uncritical reliance on pupils possessing instinctive powers of self-expression. Much has been undertaken in the past in the name of personal expressiveness which is neither personal nor expressive. The structured study of the great variety of ideas and technologies of contemporary art and design has been neglected, and insufficient attention has been given to the progressive development of key skills.

The programme of study emphasizes the need to teach a range of art, craft, and design techniques. At Key Stage 1, for example:

Pupils should be introduced to the work of artists, craftspeople and designers, *e.g. drawing, painting, printmaking, photography, sculpture, ceramics, textiles, graphic design, architecture*, in order to develop their appreciation of the richness of our diverse cultural heritage. The selection should include work in a variety of genres and styles from:

a   the locality;
b   the past and present;
c   a variety of cultures, Western and non-Western

and pupils should be given the opportunity to:

a   record responses, including observations of the natural and made environment;

b   gather resources and materials, using them to stimulate and develop ideas;

c   explore and use two- and three-dimensional media, working on a variety of scales;

d   review and modify their work as it progresses;

e   develop understanding of the work of artists, craftspeople and designers, applying knowledge to their own work;

f   respond to and evaluate art, craft and design, including their own and others' work.

This second list of processes and skills is similarly expressed at Key Stage 3 although the outcomes would have been developed and the content of the curriculum changed. At Key Stage 3 pupils must examine works from the Classical, Medieval, Renaissance, and Post-Renaissance periods, as well as works from the nineteenth and twentieth centuries. This is, therefore, an art appreciation as well as practical aspect to the curriculum.

Music

Music education has always featured significantly in the life of schools. Many people will remember the 'recorder group' of their primary schools and the rather more formal 'lesson a week' that characterized secondary education. Everyone will remember school concerts or the occasional musical event during assembly. Few prize-days or presentation evenings occur without some sort of musical presentation, and many school drama events have a strong musical presence. Many thousands of children have also been able to benefit from individual instrumental tuition. Music, therefore, is more than a subject within the National Curriculum. It is part of the culture and ethos of the school and one of the touchstone issues in making a choice of schools.

The working party that prepared the proposals for music in the National Curriculum recognized its importance, but, as with the group looking at art, they were critical of wide variations in standards and provision between schools. In primary schools pupils should, they suggested, be able to develop and refine their listening-skills, to extend their experience of singing and playing, and to become involved in improvising and composing. Yet doing this depended very much on the availability of someone on the staff with specialist expertise; and where schools have such expertise, choirs, orchestras, and a high take-up of instrumental tuition is likely to be found.

At secondary level music is usually taught as a separate subject, and the working party reported that attitudes were generally positive, particularly when opportunities exist to explore a wide range of musical styles. Standards in composing were, however, variable and there was very little liaison between primary and secondary schools in terms of the way the music curriculum was operated. The working party carefully set out the way music teaching in schools should develop:

Music is so much a part of the background of everyday life that we tend to take it for granted. For many people, however, it is a powerful focus for creative energy, and one which both stimulates and guides the imagination. Music education aims to develop aesthetic sensitivity and creative ability in all pupils. For those who show high levels of motivation, commitment and skills, it can lead to employment in the music profession, the music industries and teaching. For many others, who choose different career paths, it can supply the foundation for greatly enriched leisure pursuits, both as listeners and as participants in music-making.

Within that framework, we consider that the main aim of music education in schools is to foster pupils' sensitivity to, and their understanding and enjoyment of, music, through an active involvement in listening, composing and performing. The development of musical perception and skills is dependent upon the quality, range and appropriateness of these musical experiences, as they are provided within and outside school. There are of course many different styles of music, appropriate for different purposes and offering different kinds of satisfaction and challenge; excellence may be found in any style of musical expression.

The study of music as a foundation subject should provide for the progressive development of:

- awareness and appreciation of organised sound patterns;
- skills in movement, such as motor co-ordination and dexterity, vocal skills, and skills in aural imagery (imagining and internalising sounds), acquired through exploring and organising sound;
- sensitive, analytical and critical responses to music;
- the capacity to express ideas, thoughts and feelings through music;

- awareness and understanding of traditions, idioms and musical styles from a variety of cultures, times and places; and
- the experience of fulfilment which derives from striving for the highest possible artistic and technical standards.

The statutory orders have two attainment targets:

AT1. Performing and Composing
AT2. Listening and Appraising.

The Programmes of Study have a general introduction and these use the same attainment target taken to describe what should be taught. At Key Stage 1 pupils should be given opportunities to:

a   use sounds and respond to music individually, in pairs, in groups and as a class
b   make appropriate use of I.T. to record sounds.

When performing, composing, listening and appraising, pupils should be taught to listen with concentration, exploring, internalising, *e.g. hearing in their heads*, and recognising the musical elements of:
a   pitch—high/low;
b   duration—long/short; pulse or beat; rhythm;
c   dynamics—loud/quiet/silence;
d   tempo—fast/slow;
e   timbre—quality of sound, *e.g. tinkling, rattling, smooth, ringing*;
f   texture—several sounds played or sung at the same time/one sound on its own;

and the use of the above within
g   structure—different sections, *e.g. beginning, middle, end*; repetition, *e.g. repeated patterns, melody, rhythm*.

and in performing and composing:

pupils should be taught to:
a   sing songs from memory, developing control of breathing, dynamics, rhythm and pitch;
b   play simple pieces and accompaniments, and perform short musical patterns by ear and from symbols;
c   sing unison songs and play pieces, developing awareness of other performers;
d   rehearse and share their music making;
e   improvise musical patterns, *e.g. invent and change patterns whilst playing and singing*;

f   explore, create, select and organise sounds in simple structures;
g   use sounds to create musical effects, *e.g. to suggest a machine or a walk through a forest*;
h   record their compositions using symbols, where appropriate.

At Key Stage 3 under the heading Listening and Appraising pupils should be taught to:

a   identify how resources are used in different combinations, *e.g. orchestra, choir, chamber ensemble*, and different genres, *e.g. opera, ballet, jazz*;
b   identify ways in which personal response is influenced by the environment in which the music takes place and by the use of musical elements and resources;
c   relate music to its social, historical and cultural context, using a musical score where appropriate, *e.g. identify conventions used in different times and places*;
d   identify how and why musical styles and traditions change over time and from place to place, recognising the contribution of composers and performers;
e   express and justify opinions and preferences, using musical knowledge and vocabulary.

At all stages the curriculum should include music in a variety of styles from the very diverse cultural heritage of contemporary Britain.

Physical education

PE tends to attract very contrasting responses from children. For some, stimulated and enthused by individual or team sports, it can be the high point of the curriculum. For others it can be just the reverse, particularly where cross-country runs and compulsory showers become part of the experience! The more punishing approach, however, is becoming an increasingly rare experience; PE teachers now embrace a very different idea of the subject. The National Curriculum is much more than forward and backward rolls, jumping the horse, or scaling a rope. Look, for example, at what the working group that set out the first proposals said physical education should seek to achieve:

Physical Education educates young people in and through the use and knowledge of the body and its movement. It:
- develops physical competence and enables pupils to engage in worthwhile physical activities;
- promotes physical development and teaches pupils to value the benefits of participation in physical activity while at school and throughout life;
- develops artistic and aesthetic understanding within and through movement, and
- helps to establish self-esteem through the development of physical confidence and helps pupils to cope with both success and failure in competitive and co-operative physical activities.

Physical Education also contributes to:
- the development of problem solving skills;
- the development of inter-personal skills; and
- the forging of links between the school and the community, and across cultures.

The purposes, it is important to note, are directed towards individual development and the report was at pains to separate out sport or games from the learning that is associated with physical education. Sport can, of course, help to fulfil some of the aims of a full programme of PE, but the two should not be seen as synonymous.

In PE the National Curriculum is defined in terms of just one attainment target. The central importance of *activity* in all its forms is stressed.

At Key Stage 1 three areas of activity are described: games, gymnastics, and dance. At Key Stages 2 and 3 three more are added: athletics, outdoor and adventurous activities, and swimming.

Swimming is now a compulsory part of all pupils' curriculum. Here is what the expectations are at each of the key stages: Pupils should be taught:

Key stage 2

a to swim unaided, competently and safely, for at least 25 metres;
b to develop confidence in water, and how to rest, float and adopt support positions;
c a variety of means of propulsion using either arms or legs or both, and how to develop effective and efficient swimming strokes on the front and the back;
d the principles and skills of water safety and survival;

Key stage 3

a two recognised strokes, one on the front and one on the back;
b a variety of water-based activities, *e.g. personal survival, games, synchronised swimming;*
c to apply and evaluate the principles and practice of rescue and resuscitation in water-based activities;
d two further recognised strokes;
e to apply techniques for starting, turning and finishing;

Key stage 4

a the rules for competition, and how to prepare for, and participate in, races in the various sprint, distance, medley and team events;
b to develop further the application and evaluation of the principles and practice of rescue and resuscitation in water-based activities;
c to develop, apply and evaluate their skills in selected water-based activities.

Of course in swimming some children will from a much earlier age have succeeded at the highest level. The National Curriculum does, however, provide an expectation for what all pupils can achieve, and when fully implemented it should raise the general standards of physical activity significantly.

For pupils, mostly in the secondary school, who are working at Key Stages 3 and 4, an element of choice has been introduced into the curriculum by subdividing the activity areas into links under the title of Units A and B. There is a strong emphasis on the health dimension to physical activity as well as to the skills and competitive opportunities.

Physical education has been one of the less controversial areas of the National Curriculum. There remain, however, a number of issues that regularly attract media attention. The contribution of PE to the general health of the country, and health education specifically, is often discussed. If schools can develop a positive attitude to exercise and activity, the benefits could be considerable. How appropriate PE is to the development of boys and girls is also an issue. Should they be taught together or separately? What should be our attitude towards girls' rugby teams? Should we try to convince boys of the value of contemporary dance? Finally, a third issue relates to the performance of national teams. If the national football team fails to qualify for the World Cup, or if the Ashes are continuously lost to the Australians, are the schools to blame?

It is inevitable that these debates will continue. Significantly, however, the National Curriculum has acknowledged a broad interpretation of what physical education represents. This, in itself, offers an entitlement to opportunity for young people to join personal motivation and satisfaction in a broader range of activity than has traditionally been the case.

Information technology

There is one final part of the National Curriculum which is set out in detail within the statutory orders but which is not seen as a subject in its own right. Information technology (IT) now features in the vast majority of subjects. Schools must plan this carefully, and they have a responsibility to ensure, for example, that pupils are taught to use IT equipment and software with confidence and purpose (at Key Stage 1), assess the value of IT in their working practices (at Key Stage 2), become critical and largely autonomous users of IT (at Key Stage 3), and understand the most advanced features of IT (at Key Stage 4). This is statutory for all key stages in England. In Wales there is no statutory requirement for IT at Key Stage 4.

This is a significant and innovative feature of the National Curriculum. It is an area that few parents will have experienced in schools, although many will be using IT in their work. Costs of hardware and software have gone down in recent years and many homes will have the IT capability that a few years ago existed only in the most advanced of universities and commercial and industrial settings. Parents can assist their children in this area as in all aspects of the curriculum. It is important, for example, to encourage children to go *beyond games*, to use IT as a means of communication and to solve problems. This can begin from the earliest years through keeping a pocket-money account or planning a holiday. Given the particular importance and newness of this area, the programme of study for each of the key stages is printed in chart form below:

Information Technology

PROGRAMMES OF STUDY

COMMON REQUIREMENTS

• **Access**

The programme of study for each key stage* should be taught to the great majority of pupils in the key stage, in ways appropriate to their abilities.

For the small number of pupils who may need the provision, material may be selected from earlier or later key stages where this is necessary to enable individual pupils to progress and demonstrate achievement. Such material should be presented in contexts suitable to the pupil's age.

Appropriate provision should be made for pupils who need to use:

- means of communication other than speech, including computers, technological aids, signing, symbols or lip-reading;
- non-sighted methods of reading, such as Braille, or non-visual or non-aural ways of acquiring information;
- technological aids in practical and written work;
- aids or adapted equipment to allow access to practical activities within and beyond school.

Judgements made in relation to the level descriptions should allow for the provision above, where appropriate.

• **Use of language**

Pupils should be taught to express themselves clearly in both speech and writing and to develop their reading skills. They should be taught to use grammatically correct sentences and to spell and punctuate accurately in order to communicate effectively in written English or, when the medium is Welsh, in written Welsh.

• **Information technology capability**

Information technology (IT) capability is characterised by an ability to use effectively IT tools and information sources to analyse, process and present information, and to model, measure and control external events. This involves:

- using information sources and IT tools to solve problems;
- using IT tools and information sources, such as computer systems and software packages, to support learning in a variety of contexts;
- understanding the implications of IT for working life and society.

Pupils should be given opportunities, where appropriate, to develop and apply their IT capability in their study of National Curriculum subjects.

• **The Curriculum Cymreig**

In Wales, pupils should be given opportunities, where appropriate, in their study of information technology to develop and apply their knowledge and understanding of the cultural, economic, environmental, historical and linguistic characteristics of Wales.

• **Referencing**

The numbers and letters throughout the programmes of study are for referencing purposes only and do not necessarily indicate a particular teaching sequence or hierarchy of knowledge, understanding and skills.

* In Wales, there are no statutory requirements for IT at Key Stage 4

KEY STAGE 1 PROGRAMME OF STUDY

> Pupils should be taught to use IT equipment and software confidently and purposefully to communicate and handle information, and to support their problem solving, recording and expressive work.

- **1. Pupils should be given opportunities to:**

  a use a variety of IT equipment and software, including microcomputers and various keyboards, to carry out a variety of functions in a range of contexts;

  b explore the use of computer systems and control technology in everyday life;

  c examine and discuss their experiences of IT, and look at the use of IT in the outside world.

Pupils should be taught to:

- **2. Communicating and handling information**

  a generate and communicate their ideas in different forms, using text, tables, pictures and sound;

  b enter and store information;

  c retrieve, process and display information that has been stored.

- **3. Controlling and modelling**

  a recognise that control is integral to many everyday devices;

  b give direct signals or commands that produce a variety of outcomes, and describe the effects of their actions;

  c use IT-based models or simulations to explore aspects of real and imaginary situations.

KEY STAGE 2 PROGRAMME OF STUDY

> Pupils should be taught to extend the range of IT tools that they use for com-
> munication, investigation and control; become discerning in their use of IT; select
> information, sources and media for their suitability for purpose; and assess the
> value of IT in their working practices.

- **1. Pupils should be given opportunities to:**

    a use IT to explore and solve problems in the context of work across a variety
    of subjects;

    b use IT to further their understanding of information that they have retrieved
    and processed;

    c discuss their experiences of using IT and assess its value in their working
    practices;

    d investigate parallels with the use of IT in the wider world, consider the effects
    of such uses, and compare them with other methods.

Pupils should be taught to:

- **2. Communicating and handling information**

    a use IT equipment and software to communicate ideas and information in a
    variety of forms, incorporating text, graphs, pictures and sound, as appropri-
    ate, showing sensitivity to the needs of their audience;

    b use IT equipment and software to organise, reorganise and analyse ideas and
    information;

    c select suitable information and media, and classify and prepare information
    for processing with IT, checking for accuracy;

    d interpret, analyse and check the plausibility of information held on IT systems,
    and select the elements required for particular purposes, considering the con-
    sequences of any errors.

- **3. Controlling, monitoring and modelling**

    a create, test, modify and store sequences of instructions to control events;

    b use IT equipment and software to monitor external events;

    c explore the effect of changing variables in simulations and similar packages,
    to ask and answer questions of the 'What would happen if . . . ?' type;

    d recognise patterns and relationships in the results obtained from IT-based
    models or simulations, predicting the outcomes of different decisions that could
    be made.

KEY STAGE 3 PROGRAMME OF STUDY

> Pupils should be taught to become critical and largely autonomous users of IT, aware of the ways in which IT tools and information sources can help them in their work; understand the limitations of such tools and of the results they produce; and use the concepts associated with IT systems and software and the associated technical terms.

- **1. Pupils should be given opportunities to:**

    a use IT equipment and software autonomously;

    b consider the purposes for which information is to be processed and communicated;

    c use their knowledge and understanding of IT to design information systems, and to evaluate and suggest improvements to existing systems;

    d investigate problems by modelling, measuring and controlling, and by constructing IT procedures;

    e consider the limitations of IT tools and information sources, and of the results they provide, and compare their effectiveness and efficiency with other methods of working;

    f discuss some of the social, economic, ethical and moral issues raised by IT.

Pupils should be taught to:

- **2. Communicating and handling information**

    a use a range of IT equipment and software efficiently to create good quality presentations for particular audiences, integrating several forms of information;

    b select appropriate IT equipment and software to fulfil their specific purposes;

    c be systematic in their use of appropriate search methods to obtain accurate and relevant information from a range of sources;

    d collect and amend quantitative and qualitative information for a particular purpose, and enter it into a data-handling package for processing and analysis;

    e interpret, analyse and display information, checking its accuracy and questioning its plausibility.

- **3. Controlling, measuring and modelling**

    a plan, develop, test and modify sets of instructions and procedures to control events;

    b use a system that responds to data from sensors and explain how it makes use of feedback;

    c use IT equipment and software to measure and record physical variables;

    d explore a given model with a number of variables and create models of their own, in order to detect patterns and relationships;

    e modify the rules and data of a model, and predict the effects of such changes;

    f evaluate a computer model by comparing its behaviour with data gathered from a range of sources.

KEY STAGE 4 PROGRAMME OF STUDY

In England, the Key Stage 4 Programme of Study is statutory.
In Wales, there are no statutory requirements for IT at Key Stage 4.

Pupils should be taught to develop greater responsibility for their use of IT; work competently and effectively with a range of IT tools and materials, acquiring an understanding of their more advanced features; and reflect critically on their own and others' use of IT.

- **1. Pupils should be given opportunities to:**

  a develop further as autonomous users of IT, broadening and consolidating their knowledge, skills and understanding;

  b select from a range of IT tools and information sources those that are appropriate for a variety of tasks;

  c learn to operate unfamiliar systems and acquire an understanding of their more advanced features;

  d apply and continue to develop their IT skills in order to enhance their work in a variety of subject or vocational areas;

  e recognise the impact of new technologies on methods of working in the outside world, and on social, economic, ethical and moral issues.

Pupils should be taught to:

- **2. Communicating and handling information**

  a use IT to handle and communicate information in a variety of contexts;

  b use IT to enhance their own learning and the quality of their work;

  c increase their understanding of the social, ethical, moral and economic impact of technology on their lives;

  d analyse the requirements of a specific task, taking into account the information required and the purpose for which it is needed, and decide how the information will be presented and interpreted.

- **3. Controlling, measuring and modelling**

  a apply their existing knowledge and understanding of measurement, control and modelling to a wide variety of contexts, in a range of subject or vocational areas;

  b understand the uses, advantages and disadvantages of particular modelling techniques.

Special Needs

Many people are now aware that the school provision for children with special needs underwent revolutionary changes in the 1980s and early 1990s. The impetus came from a report on the education of handicapped children and young people published in 1978 (the Warnock Report). This established clearly that educational goals should be the same for all young people, regardless of any disability they might have. In 1981 an Education Act was passed, and in the following decade children with special educational needs who had been educated separately were gradually integrated into mainstream schools. Special schools still exist, but for a very small minority of children.

The 1978 Warnock Report and the Education Acts (1981 and 1993) reflected the change in social attitudes to disability that has characterized the latter part of the twentieth century. Segregation in special schools had done little for the progress or self-esteem of many children; nor did it help promote sensitive, informed, and caring understanding on the part of children or adults without disability.

Children who experience particular difficulties may be assessed and where appropriate become the subject of what is termed a statement. With the agreement and, following the 1993 Act, the full involvement of parents throughout the process, this will be drawn up by a group of professionals from a variety of backgrounds (educational psychologists, doctors, social workers, and teachers). When the statement is complete the school may receive extra resources to support the child's education. It will certainly be required to follow the recommendation made in the statement. In drawing up the statement, careful consideration will be given to the extent to which the child can follow the National Curriculum. The Schools Curriculum and Assessment Authority has made it very clear that children with special needs should have maximum access to all aspects of the National Curriculum. Only when this is clearly impossible will the requirements be waived (the rather unfriendly technical term *disapplication* is used in the legislation to describe this process), Whatever the outcome, the curriculum programme for each child will need to be broad, balanced, and rich in opportunities for a full range of activities.

There will also be pupils in schools who are not the subject of a statement but who still have special educational needs. They too will need support. These children include those who follow the full National Curriculum programme of their peers but require specialist help with reading or numbers, and those who have been temporarily withdrawn from all or parts of the National Curriculum. This latter situation will only occur in a few circumstances, for example:

- where pupils have arrived from such a different educational system that they require a period of adjustment to the National Curriculum;
- where pupils have had spells in hospital, been educated at home, or been excluded from school and need time to adjust;
- where pupils have temporary severe emotional problems (perhaps because of a family crisis) and need special arrangements.

The headteacher, with the agreement of the governors, has the power to make what is called a temporary 'general direction' to waive part of the National Curriculum. This cannot be done for longer than six months. The school is still responsible for the child's curriculum and it must ensure that a broad and balanced range of activities is offered.

All schools are now required to draw up policies for teaching and supporting children with special needs. School prospectuses and governors' statements about the curriculum will include a reference to the approach adopted. Governors must report once a year to parents and this report must include a statement on the school's special-needs policy. In recent years there has been a marked shift not only towards teaching special-needs children in mainstream schools, but also towards teaching them in ordinary classes. OFST-ED inspections particularly address special-needs provision. Teachers with particular responsibilities for special-needs children are there-fore more likely to be working alongside their colleagues, giving group and individual support, rather than in their own specialist room or department.

The Department for Education has now published a national Code of Practice on the Identification and Assessment of children with Special Educational Needs and schools must work to this document in establishing and developing policies and practice in this area. The Code sets out five stages of need, from Stage 1 where needs should be dealt with at school level to Stage 5 when a child would be the subject of a statement. At Stage 3 expert help from outside the school, for example, educational psychologists, must be drawn in. The Code is a lengthy document and has been widely welcomed. A short guide for parents is available and schools will have copies.

All the National Curriculum statutory orders now open with a statement on access to the curriculum, and this is particularly rel-evant to children with special needs:

The programme of study for each key stage should be taught to the great majority of pupils in the key stage, in ways appropriate to their abilities.

For the small number of pupils who may need the provision, materi-al may be selected from earlier or later key stages where this is neces-sary to enable individual pupils to progress and demonstrate achievement. Such material should be presented in contexts suitable to the pupil's age.

Appropriate provision should be made for pupils who need to use:
- means of communication other than speech, including computers, technological aids, signing, symbols or lip-reading;
- non-sighted methods of reading, such as Braille, or non-visual or non-aural ways of acquiring information;
- technological aids in practical and written work;
- aids or adapted equipment to allow access to practical activities with-in and beyond school.

Appropriate provision should be made for pupils with hearing impair-ment, who need to use equipment and resources that visually record and display sounds.

Judgements made in relation to the end of key stage descriptions should allow for the provision above, where appropriate.

Teachers, governors, and parents should consider carefully the sorts of issues that inform the development of a special-needs policy for the curriculum. In one of the first national documents on this issue (*A Curriculum For All*) schools were asked to develop responses to a number of questions. Examples included:

- Can the tasks and activities for any one attainment level be chosen and presented to enable children with a wide range of attainments to experience success? For instance, emphasis on oral rather than written work will help some pupils with learning difficulties.
- Can activities be matched to pupils' differing paces and styles of learning, interests, capabilities, and previous experience; can time and order of priority be allocated accordingly?
- Can the activities be broken down into a series of small and achievable steps for pupils who have marked learning difficulties?
- Will the activities stretch pupils of whom too little may have been expected in the past? These pupils are likely to include some with physical, sensory, or other impairment who are high attainers.
- Can a range of communication methods be used with pupils with language difficulties?
- Will the purpose of the activities and the means of achieving them be understood and welcomed by pupils with learning difficulties?

The school environment plays an important role in developing the learning of all pupils, but it is especially important for children with special needs. The layout of the classroom, the capacity to change the way pupils are grouped, the provision of information technology and other resources, and the encouragement of co-operative approaches to learning amongst pupils can all support the integration of children with special needs into the curriculum, and stimulate the their capacity to learn.

The advice in *A Curriculum for All* gives numerous ideas and examples of how subject-teaching in the National Curriculum can be sensitive to children with special needs. For example,

- *Use of language*: 'Without water human beings are unable to survive' could become 'People need water to live.'
- *Practical activities*: Pupils may be given paper for folding into a windmill shape. Those with learning difficulties might need to have the shape printed on the sheet with the folds marked. For a visually impaired pupil the lines can be indented in the paper with pressure from a ball pen or a spur-wheel available from the Royal National Institute for the Blind (RNIB). This creates an embossed shape on the reverse side of the paper which the child can feel. Even with extra

help like this, pupils will still need close guidance by the class teacher and classroom helpers.

- *Classroom method*: Teachers will need to find ways to help those pupils who have specific learning difficulties in reading and writing to make use of their oral strengths (for example, use of tape-recorder and word-processor) and to ensure that evaluation and feedback on work are not over-dominated by hand-written products.

It is important that everyone involved, professionals, parents, and governors, be fully aware of the statutory responsibilities and regulations in formulating and developing policies. For example, the statutory orders for Key Stage 1 in English allow pupils to be exempted from the 'Handwriting' requirements if they need to use a non-sighted form of writing or if they have such a degree of physical disability that the attainment target is impossible. This has implications for the way in which National Curriculum achievements are assessed and reported to parents. SCAA gives specific advice on how the regulations should be interpreted, and local education authorities also have officers and advisers who monitor the way the National Curriculum is taught in schools and can give individual advice to parents and teachers of children with special educational needs.

8 Parents and Governors

Parents

Parents are entitled to a range of information about the school curriculum in general and the progress their child is making through that curriculum. This entitlement dates back to legislation as long ago as 1981, but most of the regulations followed the passing of the Education Reform Act in 1988.

Those who want to find out as much as possible about a school curriculum can:

1. obtain copies of the statutory orders for each of the subjects: every school must have these available for parents to look through, and they can also be purchased through HMSO (see Further Reading);
2. ask for a copy of the school prospectus, which should contain the governors' statement of curriculum aims for the school;
3. look through the school prospectus for the following information which must be included:
    *   a summary of the content and organization of that part of the curriculum relating to sex-education (where it is offered);
    *   the hours spent on teaching during the normal school week, including religious education, but excluding the statutory daily act of collective worship, registration, and breaks (including lunch);
    *   the dates of school terms and half-terms for the next school year;
    *   a summary of each year group, indicating the content of the school curriculum and how it is organized, including

in particular how National Curriculum subjects and religious education are organized, what other subjects and cross-curricular themes are included in the curriculum for all pupils, what optional subjects are available, and how choices among them are constrained;

- a list of the external qualifications (certificates) offered by examining bodies in specific subjects, approved under section 5 of the Education Reform Act, for which courses of study are provided for pupils of compulsory school age;
- the names of the syllabuses associated with the qualifications; a list of the external qualifications (certificates) offered by examining bodies in specific subjects, and the names of the associated syllabuses, offered to those beyond compulsory school age;
- details of any careers education provided, and the arrangements made for work experience;
- information about how to make a complaint, according to arrangements established under section 23 of the Education Reform Act;
- how to see and, where appropriate, acquire the documents to be made available under the Regulations.

4. ask to see any schemes of work currently used by teachers in the school, or any syllabuses followed, whether for public examinations or otherwise.

These four sources of information must be made available to parents under the new regulations. In addition, any *entitled* person must have access to curricular records and any other educational records relating to a registered pupil and kept at the school. An entitled person is defined as a parent of a pupil under 16, both the parent and the pupil when the person is aged 16 or 17, and the pupil only when aged 18 or over.

Access to the records must be provided within fifteen school days of the request being made, and there is a system for a written request for corrections if the records are considered to be inaccurate. The records should indicate how each child is progressing in all areas of the National Curriculum.

These developments were reinforced in October 1991 by the publication of the Parent's Charter. This reiterated some of the regulations already in force but it also added a full range of information to which parents could have access. The charter includes five documents which parents have a right to receive:

- an annual report on the child;
- regular reports from independent inspectors;
- performance tables for all local schools;
- a prospectus or brochure about the school;
- an annual governors' report on the school.

It also gives fuller specification to the form that the annual report to parents should take:

- comments on the pupil's progress in National Curriculum subjects;
- the pupil's level of attainment in each subject at the end of each key stage following statutory assessment at ages 7, 11, 14, and 16;
- results of other examinations or tests taken during the year;
- comments on the pupil's achievements in other subjects beside those of the National Curriculum and in other activities;
- comparison between the individual's results in examinations and national tests and those of others in the same group, and the national average;
- a comment from the headteacher or class teacher on general progress and attendance record;
- an indication of the person to whom the parent should talk to discuss the report, and details of how to fix an appointment.

So far the legal requirements have been described. Most, if not all, schools will be making arrangements that go beyond this. For example:

- There may be special parents' evenings when the curriculum for a particular subject or one-year group is described in detail.
- Schools may provide visiting 'days' or 'times' when parents can drop in and observe classes. Timetable structures often make this easier at primary than secondary school, although at the secondary level parents' evenings may include 'sample' lessons with parents as pupils!
- The child's individual class teacher or tutor may make

arrangements for contact at times when parents have particular concerns or queries.

- Annual reports to parents may be linked to an individual interview with the class teacher or tutor. At secondary level, subject specialists may also be available to help interpret the reports.

A good school welcomes parental interest and enquiries. It is, of course, important to remember just how busy a good school is. To turn up without warning and demand to see all the documentation described in this section would be unreasonable. It is also important to remember the importance of establishing the best possible relationship with schools and teachers. Some parents (and even some governors) have been known to approach the school with an element of suspicion, perhaps giving the impression of trying to catch someone out. On the other hand, parents should not be too meek in seeking out information or in ensuring that their children are receiving the full range of curriculum opportunities to which they are entitled. If anyone really feels that the school is not fulfilling the letter of the law, then section 23 of the Education Reform Act ensures that each LEA must establish arrangements for considering complaints from parents. Every school prospectus, as has been shown, must contain information about how a complaint can be made.

Beyond all this, parents are now encouraged to take an interest in their child's progress through the curriculum. If, from the earliest age, children are made to feel that the different school subjects and topics are of intrinsic interest, this will have great advantages for their later experience of schooling. Model-making kits, books, atlases, and colourful magazines all help with this. Some special National Curriculum books and materials have appeared on the market. It would be wrong to be critical of all of these, but two things should be remembered:

- the National Curriculum is not an examination. Books that are really only an 'exam crib' should be treated with caution;
- the National Curriculum should not become burdensome to the child; this would be a severe blow to motivation and probably attainment. Any work at home should grow naturally from the school curriculum, and not be a means of

forcing or pushing the child further than he or she needs to be at a particular stage.

Governors

Many of the concerns of parents and governors overlap. Governors have a particular responsibility to be responsive to the needs and interests of parents. They also have legal responsibilities for implementing the National Curriculum, and these must be clear to anyone taking the role of governor.

Every school has a governing body. The size varies with the size of the school, but it is usually made up of a combination of parents, teachers, LEA appointees, and co-opted governors. Headteachers have the choice of becoming governors, and the vast majority choose to join the governing board with full voting rights. All governors are appointed for a four-year term.

Under their curriculum responsibilities, governors must:

- ensure that the National Curriculum is implemented within the total school curriculum. They are also responsible for ensuring that provision of religious education meets the requirements of the law;
- prepare a school statement of policy, bearing in mind the LEA's curriculum statement policy and ensuring, of course, that all the requirements of the National Curriculum are met;
- determine the length of the school day and teaching sessions, within the data set by LEAs for terms and half-terms;
- receive complaints from parents about the way the National Curriculum is working. If governors fail to satisfy the parent then the LEA-agreed arrangements for complaints may be brought into operation;
- agree and determine school financial expenditure, much of which will be linked to the implementation of the National Curriculum;
- hold an annual meeting to which a written report of the work of the school and the activities of the governors must be presented—the report must be distributed at least two weeks prior to the meeting. Examination, and where appropriate

National Curriculum assessment, results must be included in
the report;

- submit annually to the LEA information about the educational provision they are making for pupils, including points where the National Curriculum has been modified for certain pupils;

- submit information about curriculum modifications for pupils who are the subject of a statement (see Chapter 7).

In schools that have opted for grant-maintained status governors are not required to make the same links with LEAs that are set out above. In carrying out their duties, however, governors in all schools will work closely with the headteacher and other teachers. The statement of curriculum policy, for example, may be drawn up following discussion of a draft prepared by the headteacher and other members of staff and by reference to the curriculum policy of the local education authority. The annual return of information about the curriculum will almost certainly be drawn up by teaching staff. If a pupil, perhaps though illness or because of behaviour difficulties, has to have the National Curriculum modified for a period of time, the governors will be advised by the headteacher. Governors do have significant responsibilities for the curriculum, however, and they will need to become conversant with the terminology of the particular approach adopted by the school. Most schools now arrange for governors to spend time in classes. At secondary level particular governors may take an interest in different parts of the curriculum, although they should also be aware of the strategies adopted for whole-curriculum planning. Governors have an important role to play in making sure that curriculum arrangements are described clearly to parents. Technical and obscure professional terminology should be avoided. To fulfil these responsibilities, governors need to have more than a cursory understanding of the issues involved.

9 Revising the National Curriculum

The introduction of the National Curriculum was fraught with difficulties. Teachers were resistant to some of the proposals. Politicians argued over many aspects of the statutory orders. The place of grammar in English, the weight to be given to British history, and what constituted a music curriculum all received widespread media attention. Most significantly of all, the first attempts to produce fair forms of tasks and assessment were failures.

Despite this, the significant majority of parents and teachers were, and are, in favour of the principle of a National Curriculum. And many other countries are looking with interest at the way it develops. Teachers had to put in a tremendous amount of effort to launch the new programmes and implement what seemed an ever-changing system of assessment. Primary teachers in particular had a highly complex task to perform in integrating the subject orders into the well-planned primary curriculum.

In 1993, responding to the weight of concern about the first proposals, a major review was carried out by Sir Ron Dearing, who at the time chaired the Schools Curriculum and Assessment Authority. The revised National Curriculum, considerably slimmed down and simplified, was introduced in September 1995. At the time the government gave an undertaking, not to change the orders in any significant way for five years. The changes were so extensive that teachers have had to go through a further, completely new planning cycle, and so a first run-through of a settled National Curriculum will not be complete until the year 2000!

10 Controversial and Unresolved Issues

The National Curriculum has now been established for the five years between 1995 and the year 2000. There is now a much stronger consensus about its focus and structure than when it was first introduced in 1988. Given the scale and importance of the whole undertaking, difficulties still remain. This section does not attempt to do justice to all the unresolved issues surrounding the National Curriculum; rather, ten issues that government, parents, and teachers may become involved with are listed, and the Further Reading (below) provides the means for investigating each one further.

Fitting everything in

One of the biggest difficulties with the National Curriculum was its overcrowding, within subjects and across the curriculum as a whole. The review carried out in the early 1990s was critical and commented on this.

The national curriculum is defined at present in a detailed and prescriptive way. This level of prescription stemmed no doubt from the belief that the national curriculum, if it is to raise standards, should map the ground to be covered in an unambiguous way. But teachers have found that the degree of detail and prescription intrudes into the proper exercise of professional judgement, and tends to diminish the quality of the educational experience they can offer.

In primary schools, they felt that children should be allowed to pursue individual interests, follow up projects, and so on. This was equally true at secondary level, where it will be important to ensure a healthy take-up of a second foreign language and subjects such as drama and dance. The detailed and prescriptive way in which the National Curriculum was set out required so much attention that other subjects became neglected. This was particularly true at Key Stage 4, when a full programme of National Curriculum GCSE subjects left little room for studying any other subject.

The changes introduced in 1995 went some way to answering these criticisms but some teachers still talk of over-prescription. It still takes a great deal of work at the national and school level to plan a whole curriculum at each of the four stages. This is likely to be one of the most important educational issues for debate and development in the second part of the 1990s.

Subjects missed out of the National Curriculum

One of the criticisms of the National Curriculum is that the subjects are rather old-fashioned. Apart from design technology, the list could have come out of a 1950s grammar school (or even one of the new secondary schools in the early 1900s). Although the National Curriculum does not have to be taught in subjects, it does have a strong influence on the way people think and the way each school's curriculum is planned. Many people point particularly to the way in which art and music are stipulated, as opposed to the more broadly based approach (adopted by most primary and an increasing number of secondary schools) of creative arts generally. In other words, are the arts going to become the low-status part of the National Curriculum? Home economics teachers are also concerned about the status and importance of their subject if it is subsumed within design technology.

Perhaps one of the most pressing issues is how to ensure that the curriculum at Key Stage 4 provides opportunities for vocational and subject-based study. The 1988 plans gave little scope for this. The introduction of more flexible subject requirements at Key Stage 4 means that schools can now begin to plan a curriculum which takes account of vocational interests and allows some planning across the 14–18 or 19 age-range rather than just to 16.

Planning across the curriculum

Many of the areas left out of the National Curriculum, for example, environmental education, economic awareness, and citizenship, must now be taught with and across the programmes of study and attainment targets of the subjects. These topics involve highly significant issues for the last decade of the twentieth century. How are schools ensuring that they are covered? Are they really seen to be important by teachers, parents, and pupils?

Dated content

England and Wales now have some of the most detailed curriculum requirements in the world. Knowledge in many areas, particularly in science and technology, evolves rapidly. Taking another perspective, some people have argued that many parts of the statutory curriculum (for example, in history) are culturally biased and need modification. Does the five-year moratorium on change allow time to keep subjects up to date and responsive to changing social attitudes and values?

Recording achievement

In Chapters 2 and 4 the question of achievement was discussed at some length. There is still a long way to go in providing assessment evidence that is reliable and fair and gives useful information to teachers, pupils, and parents, and that can be used in judging how well the school as a whole is doing. Some experts say that different forms of assessment should be used for different purposes. For example, it is necessary to assess in one way to give detailed information on how well an individual pupil is doing, and in another way to measure how well a school, or all the pupils in a particular year, are progressing. Other people argue for a more informed approach. Much of the debate is technical, and in the early years the National Curriculum became embroiled in an over-simplistic and very political 'pro-testing/anti-testing' debate. The issue will not be resolved quickly or easily, and the national assessment system is still at an experimental stage.

Giving parents information

As Chapter 8 described, parents now have the right to a range of information about the curriculum and their child's progress. This ought to be seen as a minimum requirement, and not as the full extent of the obligation. In good schools parents are given information about a wide variety of curriculum plans and activities. They are also shown how their help and encouragement can ensure that children progress with confidence and security. Finding the best ways of doing this, and making school–parent links a national part of any child's education, still represent a challenge to school organization, and new ways and approaches are sought. Finding ways of making public information on tests and examinations fair and reliable is also a challenge. Comparing schools simply on the basis of test or examination results is now widely accepted as unfair. Schools serving more socially and economically advantaged areas clearly have a head start. One way is to look at the progress children make after entering a school. This can say something about the value that individual schools add to a child's education. This is a complex area, one likely to be a focus of educational debate for some time.

Equal opportunities issues

There is now considerable evidence to show that certain groups of pupils are disadvantaged within the school curriculum. Research evidence suggests, for example, that girls are often disadvantaged by the design of tests and examinations. Children with certain special needs do not always receive the support they should. Ethnicity is also an issue in which inequalities have been extensively researched. Schools are expected to monitor the curriculum and assessment results, and to try to remedy any difficulties that arise. How this is done, however, is controversial and open to a variety of different approaches.

Resources

Many teachers argue that insufficient attention has been paid to the resources needed for the National Curriculum. The statutory orders in some instances involve the wholesale revision of textbooks. Schools find it difficult to restock across a whole subject. There are also the costs of new equipment for subjects such as design technology, and especially for information technology. The science programme involves primary schools in ongoing consumable supplies that were not previously required. Finally there is the issue of staff training, and whether the money conceded by the government is sufficient to meet these needs.

Teacher shortages and skills

Now that every school has to provide a National Curriculum, the problems of providing appropriately qualified teachers are clearly revealed. Finding sufficient numbers of science, design and technology, or modern language teachers is proving difficult in many parts of the country. There are shortages too in other subjects, such as mathematics and even English. In some years, particularly when the economy is growing, insufficient numbers of people come forward to train in these areas, and the difficulties, therefore, cannot be resolved quickly. There are also some shortages that are important, but less easy to observe. Some teachers of subjects such as English and mathematics have no qualifications in the subject. It is important to ensure that they are receiving adequate additional training, support, and guidance. Similarly, in primary schools where teachers have to teach across the range of the National Curriculum, it is highly unlikely that any teacher will have sufficient grasp of all the subjects. Training and help are needed (and primary teachers rarely have the 'non-contact' time usually allocated to secondary-school teachers). It is a challenge to provide the necessary support without too much disruption to existing classes.

Teaching to the test

One of the main worries about a prescribed curriculum and national tests is the extent to which teaching will focus on the tests and neglect other equally important areas. Not all the subjects of the National Curriculum are nationally tested. Will this give some higher status than others? And what about the best teaching and learning that can happen when an unpredictable interest develops and individuals and classes are motivated to pursue particular lines of enquiry in some depth? Will the gifted teacher and communicator be constrained by the orders? Will schools worry overmuch about children participating in trips and activities that may disrupt their National Curriculum studies but could provide experiences and memories that last a lifetime? Equally, will some parents become over-anxious and stifle that natural curiosity of children to follow an idea and lead independent of something as remote as a statutory order? These issues will need monitoring, and research and evaluation will be important throughout the 1995–2000 period.

Further Reading

Information about the National Curriculum can become dated very quickly. It is important, therefore, in looking for the statutory requirements, to purchase the relevant subject booklets or the whole National Curriculum compendium covering all subjects (there is one for each of the subjects). They can be ordered through booksellers or direct from:

HMSO
PO Box 276,
London SW8 8DT.

Each of the national councils also has an information section, producing a variety of helpful literature, including some specialist leaflets for parents and employers. The addresses are:

Schools Curriculum and Assessment Authority
Newcombe House
45 Notting Hill Gate
London W11 3JB.

SCAA Wales
Phase 2, East Buildings
Ty Glas Road
Llanishen
Cardiff CF4 5WE.

SCAA Northern Ireland
Rathgate House
Balloo Road
Bangor
County Down BT19 2PR.

Additionally, the Department for Education and Science, and the Welsh Office, publish regulations and advisory documents:

DFE
Sanctuary Buildings
Great Smith Street

Westminster
London SW1P 3BT.

DFE; Welsh Office
Crown Building
Cathays Park
Cardiff CF1 3NQ.

DFE; Northern Ireland (DENI)
Rathgate House
Balloo Road
Bangor
County Down BT19 2PR.

A number of books have now been published that describe the historical and political origins of the National Curriculum. Two authors—Denis Lawton and Clyde Chitty—have together and separately produced five interesting critical volumes;

Chitty, C. (1987), *Towards a New Education System: The Victory of the New Right?* (Falmer Press).

Lawton, D. (1989), *Education, Culture and the National Curriculum* (Hodder & Stoughton).

Lawton, D., and Chitty, C. (1988), *The National Curriculum* (Bedford Way Series, Institute of Education, University of London).

Lawton, D. (1992), *Education and Politics in the 1990s: Conflict or Consensus?* (Falmer Press).

Lawton, D. (1994), *Education Reformed* (Hodder and Stoughton).

The most authoritative account of the whole of the 1988 Education Reform Act, including the curriculum clauses, is in Stuart Maclure's *Education Reformed* (Hodder & Stoughton, 1989).

The Open University is producing a number of courses focusing on National Curriculum issues. 'Curriculum and Learning', first presented in 1991, includes text, television films, audio-cassettes, and readers, and also includes a discussion of a number of aspects of the National Curriculum. One of the readers—Bob Moon (ed.), *New Curriculum: National Curriculum* (Hodder & Stoughton, 1991)—includes a number of critical analyses of the period leading up to the implementation of the new legislation. A book on *Managing the National Curriculum*, edited by Tim Brighouse and Bob Moon, is now in a second edition and is published by Longmans.

A journal, the *Curriculum Journal*, published three times a year by Routledge for the Curriculum Association, is a valuable source of comment and analysis.

Schools and local authority advisory services will also be able to provide advice on publications which report the latest legislative developments in the National Curriculum.

List of Abbreviations

AoE	Area of Experience
APU	Assessment of Performance Unit
AT	Attainment Target
CAI	Common Assessment Instrument
CCW	Curriculum Council for Wales
CFS	Core Foundation Subject
DES	Department of Education and Science
DfE	Department for Education
FS	Foundation Subject
HMI	Her Majesty's Inspectorate
HSU	Historical Study Unit
IT	Information Technology
KAL	Knowledge about Language
LEA	Local Education Authority
LoA	Level of Attainment
MFL	Modern Foreign Languages
NC	National Curriculum
NCC	National Curriculum Council
NISEAC	Northern Ireland Schools Examination and Assessment Council
OFSTED	Office for Students in Education
PoS	Programme of Study
SAT	Standard Assessment Target
SCAA	Schools Curriculum and Assessment Authority
SDU	School-designed Unit
SEAC	Schools Examination and Assessment Council
SoA	Statement of Attainment
SO	Statutory Orders
TGAT	Task Group on Assessment and Testing

Sources and Acknowledgements

NCC (1992), *Starting out with the National Curriculum* (York).

Webb, R. (1993), *Eating the Elephant Bit by Bit: The National Curriculum at Key Stage 2* (Association of Teachers and Lecturers (ATL), London).

Dearing, R. (1993), *The National Curriculum and its Assessment: An Interim Report* (NCC and SEAC).

Cox, C. B. (1991), *Cox on Cox: An English Curriculum for the 90s* (Hodder and Stoughton).

DES (1989), *Report of the English Working Party 5–16* (The Cox Report) (HMSO, London).

DES (1988), *Report of the Committee of Inquiry into the Teaching of the English Language* (The Kingman Report) (HMSO, London).

DfE (1995), *English in the National Curriculum* (HMSO, London).

SCAA (1994), *Examples of Test Questions in English from Key Stages 1, 2 and 3.*

NCC (1991), *Mathematics: Non-statutory guidance* (York).

DfE (1995), *Mathematics in the National Curriculum* (HMSO, London).

SCAA (1994), *Examples of Test Questions in Mathematics from Key Stages 1, 2 and 3.*

DfE (1995), *Science in the National Curriculum* (HMSO, London).

SCAA (1994), *Examples of Test Questions in Science from Key Stages 2 and 3.*

NICC (1991), *Guidance Materials for History.*

CCW (1991), *Non-Statutory Guidance for History.*

DfE (1995), *History in the National Curriculum* (HMSO, London).

DfE (1995), *Geography in the National Curriculum* (HMSO, London).

DES/WO (1990), *MFL for Ages 5–16.*

DfE (1995), *MFL in the National Curriculum* (HMSO, London).

DES/WO (1991) *Art for Ages 5–16.*

DfE (1995), *Art in the National Curriculum* (HMSO, London).

DES (1992), *Music in the National Curriculum (England)* (HMSO, London).

DfE (1995), *Music in the National Curriculum* (HMSO, London).

DES (1992), *physical Education in the National Curriculum* (HMSO, London).

DfE (1995), *Physical Education in the National Curriculum* (HMSO, London).

DfE (1995), *Information Technology in the National Curriculum* (HMSO, London).

OXFORD

MORE OXFORD PAPERBACKS

This book is just one of nearly 1000 Oxford Paperbacks currently in print. If you would like details of other Oxford Paperbacks, including titles in the World's Classics, Oxford Reference, Oxford Books, OPUS, Past Masters, Oxford Authors, and Oxford Shakespeare series, please write to:

UK and Europe: Oxford Paperbacks Publicity Manager, Arts and Reference Publicity Department, Oxford University Press, Walton Street, Oxford OX2 6DP.

Customers in UK and Europe will find Oxford Paperbacks available in all good bookshops. But in case of difficulty please send orders to the Cash-with-Order Department, Oxford University Press Distribution Services, Saxon Way West, Corby, Northants NN18 9ES. Tel: 01536 741519; Fax: 01536 746337. Please send a cheque for the total cost of the books, plus £1.75 postage and packing for orders under £20; £2.75 for orders over £20. Customers outside the UK should add 10% of the cost of the books for postage and packing.

USA: Oxford Paperbacks Marketing Manager, Oxford University Press, Inc., 200 Madison Avenue, New York, N.Y. 10016.

Canada: Trade Department, Oxford University Press, 70 Wynford Drive, Don Mills, Ontario M3C 1J9.

Australia: Trade Marketing Manager, Oxford University Press, G.P.O. Box 2784Y, Melbourne 3001, Victoria.

South Africa: Oxford University Press, P.O. Box 1141, Cape Town 8000.

THE WORLD'S CLASSICS
THE WIND IN THE WILLOWS

Kenneth Grahame

The Wind in the Willows (1908) is a book for those 'who keep the spirit of youth alive in them; of life, sunshine, running water, woodlands, dusty roads, winter firesides'. So wrote Kenneth Grahame of his timeless tale of Toad, Mole, Badger, and Rat in their beautiful and benevolently ordered world. But it is also a world under siege, threatened by dark and unnamed forces—'the Terror of the Wild Wood' with its 'wicked little faces' and 'glances of malice and hatred'—and defended by the mysterious Piper at the Gates of Dawn. *The Wind in the Willows* has achieved an enduring place in our literature: it succeeds at once in arousing our anxieties and in calming them by giving perfect shape to our desire for peace and escape.

The World's Classics edition has been prepared by Peter Green, author of the standard biography of Kenneth Grahame.

'It is a Household Book; a book which everybody in the household loves, and quotes continually; a book which is read aloud to every new guest and is regarded as the touchstone of his worth.' A. A. Milne

POPULAR SCIENCE FROM
OXFORD PAPERBACKS

THE AGES OF GAIA

A Biography of Our Living Earth

James Lovelock

In his first book, *Gaia: A New Look at Life on Earth*, James Lovelock proposed a startling new theory of life. Previously it was accepted that plants and animals evolve on, but are distinct from, an inanimate planet. Gaia maintained that the Earth, its rocks, oceans, and atmosphere, and all living things are part of one great organism, evolving over the vast span of geological time. Much scientific work has since confirmed Lovelock's ideas.

In *The Ages of Gaia*, Lovelock elaborates the basis of a new and unified view of the earth and life sciences, discussing recent scientific developments in detail: the greenhouse effect, acid rain, the depletion of the ozone layer and the effects of ultraviolet radiation, the emission of CFCs, and nuclear power. He demonstrates the geophysical interaction of atmosphere, oceans, climate, and the Earth's crust, regulated comfortably for life by living organisms using the energy of the sun.

'Open the cover and bathe in great draughts of air that excitingly argue the case that "the earth is alive".' David Bellamy, *Observer*

'Lovelock deserves to be described as a genius.' *New Scientist*

THE OXFORD AUTHORS

General Editor: Frank Kermode

THE OXFORD AUTHORS is a series of authoritative editions of major English writers. Aimed at both students and general readers, each volume contains a generous selection of the best writings—poetry, prose, and letters—to give the essence of a writer's work and thinking. All the texts are complemented by essential notes, an introduction, chronology, and suggestions for further reading.

Matthew Arnold
William Blake
Lord Byron
John Clare
Samuel Taylor Coleridge
John Donne
John Dryden
Ralph Waldo Emerson
Thomas Hardy
George Herbert and Henry Vaughan
Gerard Manley Hopkins
Samuel Johnson
Ben Jonson
John Keats
Andrew Marvell
John Milton
Alexander Pope
Sir Philip Sidney
Oscar Wilde
William Wordsworth

PHILOSOPHY IN OXFORD PAPERBACKS
THE GREAT PHILOSOPHERS
Bryan Magee

Beginning with the death of Socrates in 399, and following the story through the centuries to recent figures such as Bertrand Russell and Wittgenstein, Bryan Magee and fifteen contemporary writers and philosophers provide an accessible and exciting introduction to Western philosophy and its greatest thinkers.

Bryan Magee in conversation with:

A. J. Ayer	John Passmore
Michael Ayers	Anthony Quinton
Miles Burnyeat	John Searle
Frederick Copleston	Peter Singer
Hubert Dreyfus	J. P. Stern
Anthony Kenny	Geoffrey Warnock
Sidney Morgenbesser	Bernard Williams
Martha Nussbaum	

'Magee is to be congratulated . . . anyone who sees the programmes or reads the book will be left in no danger of believing philosophical thinking is un-practical and uninteresting.' Ronald Hayman, *Times Educational Supplement*

'one of the liveliest, fast-paced introductions to philosophy, ancient and modern that one could wish for' *Universe*

OXFORD BOOKS

THE OXFORD BOOK OF ENGLISH GHOST STORIES

Chosen by Michael Cox and R. A. Gilbert

This anthology includes some of the best and most frightening ghost stories ever written, including M. R. James's 'Oh Whistle, and I'll Come to You, My Lad', 'The Monkey's Paw' by W. W. Jacobs, and H. G. Wells's 'The Red Room'. The important contribution of women writers to the genre is represented by stories such as Amelia Edwards's 'The Phantom Coach', Edith Wharton's 'Mr Jones', and Elizabeth Bowen's 'Hand in Glove'.

As the editors stress in their informative introduction, a good ghost story, though it may raise many profound questions about life and death, entertains as much as it unsettles us, and the best writers are careful to satisfy what Virginia Woolf called 'the strange human craving for the pleasure of feeling afraid'. This anthology, the first to present the full range of classic English ghost fiction, similarly combines a serious literary purpose with the plain intention of arousing pleasing fear at the doings of the dead.

'an excellent cross-section of familiar and unfamiliar stories and guaranteed to delight' *New Statesman*

ILLUSTRATED HISTORIES IN OXFORD PAPERBACKS

THE OXFORD ILLUSTRATED HISTORY OF ENGLISH LITERATURE

Edited by Pat Rogers

Britain possesses a literary heritage which is almost unrivalled in the Western world. In this volume, the richness, diversity, and continuity of that tradition are explored by a group of Britain's foremost literary scholars.

Chapter by chapter the authors trace the history of English literature, from its first stirrings in Anglo-Saxon poetry to the present day. At its heart towers the figure of Shakespeare, who is accorded a special chapter to himself. Other major figures such as Chaucer, Milton, Donne, Wordsworth, Dickens, Eliot, and Auden are treated in depth, and the story is brought up to date with discussion of living authors such as Seamus Heaney and Edward Bond.

'[a] lovely volume . . . put in your thumb and pull out plums' Michael Foot

'scholarly and enthusiastic people have written inspiring essays that induce an eagerness in their readers to return to the writers they admire' *Economist*

OXFORD POPULAR FICTION
THE ORIGINAL MILLION SELLERS!

This series boasts some of the most talked-about works of British and US fiction of the last 150 years—books that helped define the literary styles and genres of crime, historical fiction, romance, adventure, and social comedy, which modern readers enjoy.

Riders of the Purple Sage	Zane Grey
The Four Just Men	Edgar Wallace
Trilby	George Du Maurier
Trent's Last Case	E C Bentley
The Riddle of the Sands	Erskine Childers
Under Two Flags	Ouida
The Lost World	Arthur Conan Doyle
The Woman Who Did	Grant Allen

Forthcoming in October:

Olive	Dinah Craik
The Diary of a Nobody	George and Weedon Grossmith
The Lodger	Belloc Lowndes
The Wrong Box	Robert Louis Stevenson

WORLD'S CLASSICS SHAKESPEARE

'not simply a better text but a new conception of Shakespeare. This is a major achievement of twentieth-century scholarship.' Times Literary Supplement

Hamlet
Macbeth
The Merchant of Venice
As You Like It
Henry IV Part I
Henry V
Measure for Measure
The Tempest
Much Ado About Nothing
All's Well that Ends Well
Love's Labours Lost
The Merry Wives of Windsor
The Taming of the Shrew
Titus Andronicus
Troilus & Cressida
The Two Noble Kinsmen
King John
Julius Caesar
Coriolanus
Anthony & Cleopatra

OXFORD REFERENCE

THE CONCISE OXFORD COMPANION TO ENGLISH LITERATURE

Edited by Margaret Drabble and Jenny Stringer

Based on the immensely popular fifth edition of the *Oxford Companion to English Literature* this is an indispensable, compact guide to the central matter of English literature.

There are more than 5,000 entries on the lives and works of authors, poets, playwrights, essayists, philosophers, and historians; plot summaries of novels and plays; literary movements; fictional characters; legends; theatres; periodicals; and much more.

The book's sharpened focus on the English literature of the British Isles makes it especially convenient to use, but there is still generous coverage of the literature of other countries and of other disciplines which have influenced or been influenced by English literature.

From reviews of *The Oxford Companion to English Literature*:

'a book which one turns to with constant pleasure . . . a book with much style and little prejudice' Iain Gilchrist, *TLS*

'it is quite difficult to imagine, in this genre, a more useful publication' Frank Kermode, *London Review of Books*

'incarnates a living sense of tradition . . . sensitive not to fashion merely but to the spirit of the age' Christopher Ricks, *Sunday Times*